The Study of
Public Administration

Studies in Political Science

The Study of Public Administration

By Dwight Waldo

Professor of Political Science
University of California at Berkeley

RANDOM HOUSE
New York

LIBRARY OF CONGRESS CATALOG CARD NUMBER 54–12560
PRINTED IN THE UNITED STATES OF AMERICA

Preface

The aim of this publication is the understanding and appreciation of the study of public administration. It is an essay *about* public administration, not a treatise *in* public administration. Thus its perspective is broader, more general, than that of a textbook of public administration.

Put another way, this is an introduction to the textbooks and the other literature of public administration. The author hopes to convey a sense of the importance of public administration both as a human activity and an intellectual discipline; and beyond that, to introduce some important concepts and controversies involved in its study; and still beyond that, to give a view of some present frontiers of human knowledge.

Such questions as these are dealt with: What is public administration? Who should study it, and why? Where did it come from? What are the basic categories of the study or discipline? What are the interrelations of public administration as an *activity* or *process* with other activities and processes? What are the interrelations of public administration as a *study* or *discipline* with other studies and disciplines? What are contemporary trends?

Berkeley, California   DWIGHT WALDO

Contents

Contents

chapter one

What Is Public Administration?

||||||||||||||||||||||||||||||||||||||||||||||||||||||||||||||||||||||||||||||||||||||||||||||||||||||||||||||||||||||||||||||||||||||||||||||||||||||||||||||||||||||||||||||||||||||||||||||||||||

When announcement of the first atomic explosions was made there was a deep sense of awe at the power unleashed. Imagination and reason strained to comprehend what had happened and how it had been brought to pass. The sense of awe was extended to the physical science and engineering which had made this stupendous phenomenon possible.

Along with an account of the general principles of physics involved and how they had been conceived and brought to successful test by the various physicists, the government of the United States gave also an account of the human science and engineering that lay behind the achievement. In brief, a special administrative system named the Manhattan Engineer District had been set up as a subdivision of the government of the United States. The Manhattan Engineer District spent two billion dollars, under conditions of such great secrecy that comparatively few Americans knew it existed and many of its own employees did not know its purpose. It brought together thousands of variously and highly trained men, and many and rare materials and objects, from all over the earth. It built extensive facilities and created specialized subadministrative systems across the continent, tying them together in intricate ways with the administrative systems we know as business enterprises and universities. The success of the Manhattan Engineer District lies before all: its purpose was the achievement of militarily usable explosions based on nuclear fission.

Now it is a reasonable conclusion, based upon evidence, that most people regarded the atomic bomb as an achievement of physical science alone, and that the account of the Manhattan Engineer District did not make much of an impression—and has been generally forgotten. *But might we not seriously entertain another point of view: that the atomic bomb was as much an achievement on the human side as on the side of physical science?*

Not that the atomic bomb was a triumph of human morality. Perhaps the reverse was true, though judgment upon the atomic bomb cannot be dissociated from judgment upon war itself and all its modern machinery. What should be noticed is that in the perspective of history the human technology in achieving the bomb was a remarkable thing—perhaps as far removed from the social experience and imagination of any primitive people as the bomb itself from their physical experience and imagination.

To be sure, the all-but-universal judgment of the day is that our physical

1

science is progressive or mature, while our social science is backward, infantile, or adolescent. This may be true. Certainly it is true by definition if the criteria commonly used in making this judgment are accepted as the proper ones: these criteria (for example, mathematical sophistication) are the distinguishing marks of the physical sciences! But though it may be true, this judgment tends to obscure and to depreciate what we have achieved in the area of human "technology," to use a word not as hard and argumentative as science.

Because we have lived from birth in a society with an advanced technology of cooperation and have learned so much of this technology without awareness, we accept the miracles of human cooperation all about us as though they were natural or indeed inevitable. But they are not. Far from it. This technology was achieved through incalculable human industry, much systematic thought, and the flashes of inspiration of occasional geniuses. The technology of human cooperation must be learned afresh with each generation. Still fuller achievement of human purposes depends upon its extension by study and invention.

This essay is intended as an introduction to the study of one phase or aspect of human cooperation, namely, public administration. Public administration is much less than the whole process or concept of human cooperation. Those who study law, or anthropology, or economics, for example, are also studying human cooperation. There are specialized technologies within the technology of human cooperation; and there are also varying conceptual apparatuses by which study *in* or the study *of* these technologies may be approached. Public administration in our society is one of the technologies within the technology, and has its own special conceptual apparatuses in its practice and in its study.

The Problem of Definition

Logic and convention both require that we now deal more carefully with the problem of definition, What is public administration? But in truth there is no good definition of public administration. Or perhaps there are good short definitions, but no good short explanation. The immediate effect of all one-sentence or one-paragraph definitions of public administration is mental paralysis rather than enlightenment and stimulation. This is because a serious definition of the term—as against an epigrammatical definition, however witty—inevitably contains several abstract words or phrases. In short compass these abstract words and phrases can be explained only by other abstract words and phrases, and in the process the reality and importance of "it" become fogged and lost. With this warning let us consider two typical definitions:

(1) Public administration is the organization and management of men and materials to achieve the purposes of government.

(2) Public administration is the art and science of management as applied to affairs of state.

These are the ways public administration is usually defined. There is nothing wrong with such definitions—except that in themselves they do not help much in advancing understanding. Perhaps these definitions do evoke sharp concepts and vivid images in the reader's mind. But if they do not, it is better to proceed, rather than puzzle over each word, in the hope that the following explanations, descriptions, and comments will bring understanding in their train.

Administration: Art or Science?

Let us give a moment's attention to a traditional dispute in the definition of public administration, and a related source of frequent confusion in the use of the term. The conflict has concerned whether public administration is an art or science. Some students and administrators, impressed with the achievements of the natural and physical sciences, have been insistent that public administration can and should become a science in the same sense. Other students and administrators, impressed with a fluid, creative quality in actual administration, with such intangibles as judgment and leadership, have been equally insistent that public administration cannot become a science, that it is an art.

Much nonsense has resulted from the debates of the science-art controversy, but also considerable clarification of concepts and agreement on usage. It is fashionable nowadays to refer to the "art *and* science" of public administration, in the manner of the second definition above. This usage reflects a general conclusion that public administration has important aspects of *both* science and art. It reflects also, however, a desire to bypass the definitional problems, to compromise the issues by yielding to both sides, to get on with the study and practice of public administration, whatever it is. This disposition to get on is no doubt healthy, and diminishes a picayune and wasteful squabbling over words alone. But it must not be forgotten that definitions are important to fruitful study and effective action. The problem of how people are to be educated or trained for participating in public administration, for example, is one that can be solved only after a decision as to what, after all, is meant by public administration.[1]

Dual Usage of the Words *Public Administration*

A fertile source of confusion and error, closely related to the science-art controversy, is the fact that the words "public administration" have two usages. They are used to designate and delineate both (1) an area of intellectual inquiry, a discipline or study, and (2) a process or activity—that of administering public affairs. While the two meanings are of course closely related, they are nevertheless different; it is a difference similar to that between biology as the study of organisms and the organisms themselves.

Now if this distinction seems so obvious as not to warrant the making, the excuse must be that it is nevertheless a distinction often missed. It is obvious, in retrospect, that a great deal (but not all) of the controversy over whether public administration is a science or an art stemmed from failure to agree on which public administration was being discussed, the discipline or the activity. It is quickly apparent that it is easier to make the case for science on the *systematic study*, and the case for art on the *practice*, of public administration.

A student of public administration must cultivate a sharp eye for the

two usages of the term. Sometimes the meaning will be clear from definition or context, but often there is simply ambiguity and confusion. Sometimes this is true because a writer begins with a definition of public administration as a process or activity, and then proceeds, abruptly or gradually,
to use the term also to refer to the systematic study of public administration.
Sometimes too the attempt is made to embrace both meanings within the
same definition, which opens great opportunity for confusion. (Turn back
now and scrutinize the two definitions given on an earlier page. In terms
of the distinction made, is their intent clear?)

Let us confess that in attempting to clarify a distinction which is important we have made it sharper than it is in fact. To explain, recall the analogy
drawn above between biology as the study of organisms and the organisms
themselves. In this case the distinction is sharp, because while biology includes the study of man as an organism, this is but a small part of the
whole; and on the other hand, no organism except man makes much of a
study of other organisms. In the case of public administration, however,
the central concern of the study is man himself, in certain aspects and sets
of relationships; and on the other hand, much studying of public administration is carried on by men while engaged in the activities and process of
public administration. The file clerk meditating on a better filing system
for his needs, the supervisor deciding upon a new distribution of work
among his staff, the group of publicly employed social scientists making an
elaborate study of how employee morale can be maintained, are all studying public administration in some sense or aspect.

The Concept of Rational Action

The point will be made clearer by the introduction of the concept of
rational action, defined here as action correctly[2] calculated to realize given
desired goals with minimum loss to the realization of other desired goals.
We will use the concept somewhat crudely, and not pause here to consider
such interesting and important questions as whether man does wish or
should wish that all his actions be rational. We will be content for the
moment with the general observation or belief that man can and does maximize his goal achievement by taking thought, by correctly relating means
to ends.

Now public administration in *both* senses is rational action as just defined. It is action designed to maximize the realization of goals that are
public by definition. In public administration *as an activity* there is continuous calculation of the means to maximize public goals, although there is
great variation in the goal awareness, knowledge, and level of abstraction
of those engaged in the activity. A top leader may be highly trained and
spend his time and energy in a conscious and careful calculation of means
to realize given public goals. A machine-operator, on the other hand, may
not know or care about the "public" goals of the agency for which he works.
Still, the work of the machine-operator will be rational, in the sense that
it is a joining of means to ends—say, the operation of a calculating machine
for the solving of arithmetical problems. Rationality may be built into a
mechanical operation or even a profession. The task of a leader or adminis-

trator is then to relate such built-in rationality to goals which *he* seeks in such a way that these goals are maximized.

In public administration *as a study* there is also continuous calculation of the means by which public goals may be maximized. In fact this is not only a central concern of the discipline but, many would say, its sole legitimate concern. In this case too, however, there is great variation—in types of approach, in level of abstraction, in size of problem, in the generality or particularity of goals to be maximized, and so forth. Time-and-motion studies of mechanical operations, leadership decision-making, community value-structures affecting administration, auditing procedures, trade-union characteristics in public administration—these are random examples suggesting the range and variation of studies.

To visualize how study and action can blend together in the concept of rational action, let us imagine a case. Suppose that a firm of management consultants is hired on contract by a state department of public works, with the specific task of determining whether use of mechanical equipment might be made more rational. The persons assigned to the study would observe and gather data and enlist the interest and support of those employees in the department who are concerned with mechanical equipment. Eventually they would present recommendations, and these recommendations might be accepted and put into effect immediately, by the consultants working together with those in the department. In such a case, study and action are so blended that the distinction does not make much sense; and of course study is also a form of action, in the final analysis. Still, at the extreme instead of at the mean, the distinction is a very useful one. A helpful analogy is the familiar range of the spectrum: between the extreme bands are many variations and gradations.

The Meaning of Administration: Cooperative Rational Action

Up to this point we have invariably dealt with the expression *public administration* and at no time with the noun *administration* alone. An appropriate next step is to examine into the meaning of the noun alone, and then into that of the adjective.

We may proceed by analogy: Public administration is a species belonging to the genus administration, which genus in turn belongs to a family which we may call *cooperative human action.* The word *cooperative* is here defined in terms of results: human activity is cooperative if it has effects that would be absent if the cooperation did not take place. Thus—to take a frequently used illustration—when two men roll a stone which neither could roll alone, they have cooperated. The result, the rolled stone, is the test. But what if one of the two men has lent his effort unwillingly, perhaps under threat of bodily harm from the other: Is this cooperation? It is, in the meaning here assigned. Cooperation as ordinarily used suggests willingness, even perhaps enthusiasm; so we are straining the customary meaning. But the English language seems to have no word better adapted to the meaning here desired. The expression *antagonistic cooperation,* incidentally, is sometimes used in the social sciences to distinguish unwilling from willing cooperation.

We are now in a position to describe administration. Administration is a type of cooperative human effort that has a high degree of rationality. This description in turn needs some qualification.

First, administration is not necessarily the only type of human cooperation that is rational. For example, the American economic system utilizes competition between companies—antagonistic cooperation—as well as administration within them to achieve rational action in the production and distribution of economic goods.[3]

Second, there is an important question implicit in the phrase "high degree of rationality." It is well to note this question, though it cannot be discussed fully here. Whose goals or ends shall be used in assessing rationality? A little reflection will suggest that the *personal* goals of many if not all of the people in a particular administrative system are different from the formally stated goals of that system; sometimes, indeed, a product (for example, a military item) may be secret, its use unknown to many of those engaged in its manufacture. The idea of purpose or goal is essential to the definition of administration. But like quicksilver it is hard to grasp; it eludes and scatters. What shall we say is the purpose or goal of the Chevrolet Division of General Motors? In one sense certainly to make automobiles; and in another sense certainly to make profits for the stockholders. But the personal goals of all officers and employees are certainly in some senses neither of these, or at least not wholly these.[4]

Administration was described as a type of cooperative human endeavor with a high degree of rationality. What distinguishes it as a *type?* The answer depends in part upon the perspective. In one perspective the sociologist views the distinguishing characteristics as those he subsumes under the concept of *bureaucracy* (this is discussed in Chapter Five). In the conventional perspective of the student of administration these characteristics are best subsumed under the two terms *organization* and *management.*

The Nature of Organization

The terms *organization* and *management* require explanation in turn. We may begin with another analogy: organization is the anatomy, management the physiology, of administration. Organization is structure; management is functioning. But each is dependent upon and inconceivable without the other in any existing administrative system, just as anatomy and physiology are intertwined and mutually dependent in any living organism.[5] We are close to the truth, in fact, when we assert that organization and management are merely convenient categories of analysis, two different ways of viewing the same phenomena. One is static and seeks for pattern; the other is dynamic and follows movement.

More precisely, organization may be defined as *the structure of authoritative and habitual personal interrelations in an administrative system.* In any administrative system some persons give orders to others, for certain activities if not for all, and these orders or instructions are habitually followed by other persons; that is to say, some have more power than others, as evidenced by habitual command-obedience or instruction-response relationships. Usually there is an official theory or statement of what the authoritative interrelationships should be in a given administrative system. In an army unit, for example, authority is officially exercised according to the ranks (lieutenant, major, etc.) in the chain of command.

There may be considerable discrepancy, however, between the official theory or statement of authoritative interrelations and the actual, habitual exercise of authority, as evidenced by the actual giving and following of orders or directions. In truth, in any actual administrative system there is usually some discrepancy between the official theory or statement and the facts of authority as evidenced by customary action; and in some cases the official theory or statement may even be no more than a polite fiction, so far do the facts depart from it. Moreover, all or nearly all so-called subordinates, those we think of as docilely taking orders, have means or techniques for changing the behavior of their superiors—for example, the workers' slowdown, or the secretary's smile or frown. A pure one-way power relationship in human affairs is very rare, if indeed it exists. In short, the word *authoritative* in the above definition is ambiguous, since the test of authority may be either the official theory or habitual response. The definition was framed in the knowledge of this ambiguity, which is important but cannot be explored further here. In any case—this is our present point—there are more or less firm structures of personal interrelationships in an administrative system, and these we designate *organization*.

The Nature of Management

Turning to *management*, we may define it as *action intended to achieve rational cooperation in an administrative system*. An administrative system is what we are seeking to explain, and rational cooperation has already been defined. Our attention focuses, then, upon the phrase *action intended to achieve*.

Action is to be construed very broadly: *any change intended to achieve rational cooperation*. It includes self-change or activity, all effects of man upon man, and all effects of man upon nonhuman things. In the postal system, for example, action includes the deliberations of the Postmaster General on such a matter as the desirability of a system of regional postal centers, the instructions of a city postmaster in supervising his staff, and the activities of a deliverer in sorting his daily batch of mail. There is an authoritative quality involved in many of these actions: some men habitually give more instructions (which are followed) than others. Hence some writers define management in terms of direction or control. But this definition is likely to lead to an undesirable narrowing of attention.

The word *intended* in the definition has this significance: there may be a distinction between actions intended to achieve rational cooperation and actions which in fact do so. The reason for this is that in terms of given goals, actions intended to be rational may fail because not all the relevant facts and conditions are known or properly included in judgments and decisions—something which occurs in private life as well as in group activity. On the other hand, actions which are not part of any conscious rational calculation may nevertheless contribute to rational cooperation. Such actions may be sheerly accidental, or they may be actions we associate with emotions, personality, and so forth—areas beyond full scientific statement and calculation, for the present at least. *Management* is customarily used of actions *intended* to achieve rationality (and carries the presumption that the intention is usually realized), but of course an astute practitioner or student will be aware of the difference between intention and actuality and will never forget the large area still unmanageable. Incidentally, a great deal of political theory, especially in modern centuries, has concerned itself with the question of the general scope and the particular areas of human manageability. Students of administration can profit from the literature of this debate. And their findings and experience are in turn an important contribution to it.

The Meaning of Public

After this attempt at a formal definition of administration we return to the question, What is *public* administration? What qualities are signified by the adjective? How is public administration distinguished from administration in general, the species differentiated from the genus?

This is a difficult question. We might begin by defining *public* in terms of such words as *government* and *state*, as is often done. An attempt to understand these words in turn leads to an inquiry into such legal and philosophical concepts as sovereignty, legitimacy, and general welfare. These are important matters, and a student or practitioner of public administration ought to have made serious inquiry into general political theory. Such inquiry helps in understanding various phenomena, such as the coercions sometimes exercised in public administration.

Or we might take a quite different, empirical tack and attempt to define *public* simply by the test of opinion: In a particular society what functions or activities are believed to be public? This proposal has a certain crude truth or usefulness. In the United States, for example, there is certainly a general opinion that, say, the administration of military affairs is public, whereas the administration of automobile sales is private. But complications arise quickly in following this approach. People's opinions differ and are extremely hard to determine and assess (and to suggest another type of complication, the administration of automobile sales is subject to much public control, even in peacetime).

Or we might take the common-sense approach and ask simply, Does the government carry on the function or activity? For many common-sense purposes this approach is quite adequate. It will satisfy most of the purposes of the citizen, and many of those of the student and practitioner of administration. But for many purposes of study, analysis, and informed action it is quite inadequate. Even at the level of common sense it is not completely adequate. For example, there are unstable political situations in which it is difficult to identify "the government" and what is "legal." And there are borderline activities of which one is hard put to it to say whether the government carries them on or not, such are the subtleties of law and circumstances. For example, the development of atomic energy is public in the sense that the government of the United States is in charge. Indeed, there is much secrecy, and tight controls; the situation is sometimes referred to as a monopoly. Yet this program involves an intricate network of contractual relationships, not only with state and local authorities, but with private corporations and individuals. Shall we call developmental programs carried on under contract by Union Carbide and Carbon Corporation public administration?

The most fruitful approach to the meaning and significance of *public* for the student of administration is through use of certain concepts which have been developed most fully in such disciplines as sociology and anthropology. The ones suggested as being particularly useful are associated with the expressions *structural-functional analysis* and *culture*. The concepts involved in these terms are by no means completely clear and precise. About them highly technical and intense professional debates are carried on. Nevertheless they are very useful to the student of administration even if used crudely. They provide needed insight, if not firm scientific generalizations.

Clarification through Structural-Functional Analysis

Structural-functional analysis seeks the basic or enduring patterns of human needs, wants, dispositions, and expressions in *any* society. Recognizing the great diversity in human societies, it yet seeks for common denominators, for the universal grammar and syntax of collective living.

Such studies provide the basis for a meaning of *public* which one could designate universal or inherent. What is indicated—if not precisely concluded—is that institutions and activities that are associated with the identity of a group, with group life as a whole, have special coercive, symbolic, and ceremonial aspects. There is inevitably a sacred aura surrounding some aspects of government. In some societies, of course, Church and State are one, or closely joined. But even where they are officially separated, and even indeed when religion, as such, is officially proscribed by the government, the government—if it is "legitimate"—has this sacred quality. (Nationalism is, of course, often described as a secular religion.)

This approach helps us to understand the special public quality of certain functions of government, for example, the apprehension and trial at law of persons accused of crimes, and the punishment or incarceration of the convicted; the manufacture and control of money; the conduct of foreign relations; or the recruitment, training, and control of armed forces. There is about such activities a monopoly aspect, and they are heavily vested with special coercions, symbolisms, and ceremonies. It is especially in such areas of activity that when a private citizen becomes a public official we expect him to play a new role, one which gives him special powers and prestige, but also requires of him observance of certain proprieties and ceremonies.

Incidentally, though the concept of rational action seems the most useful one in defining administration, we could also use the ideas and findings of structural-functional analysis for this purpose. We could, that is to say, construct a model of what an administrative system is like as a general type, using the concepts and idiom of structural-functional analysis.

Clarification through the Concept of Culture

The concept of culture is used in the social sciences—especially anthropology and sociology—to denote the entire complex of beliefs and ways of doing things of a society. We may analyze it as follows for our purposes: By *beliefs* is meant the systems of ideas held with respect to such matters as religion, government, economics, philosophy, art, and personal interrelations. By *ways of doing things* is meant patterns of activity with respect to food, clothing, shelter, courtship and marriage, child-rearing, entertainment, aesthetic expression, and so forth. The concept implies or asserts that there is a close connection between beliefs and ways of doing things—for example, between ideas concerning art, and modes of aesthetic expression. It further implies or asserts that the various beliefs and ways of doing things in a particular culture are a system in the sense that they are dependent one upon the other, in such a way that a change in one sets off a complicated (and given the present state of our knowledge, at least, often unanticipated and uncontrollable) train of results in others. For example, the introduction of firearms or of the horse into the culture of a primitive people is likely ultimately to affect such matters as artistic expression and marriage customs.

Now the concept of culture tends somewhat to turn attention in the opposite direction from structural-functional analysis. It emphasizes the variety of human experience in society rather than the recurrent patterns. Indeed, the concept has been used in arguing the almost complete plasticity of human beings and of society—and this is the source of one of the professional controversies referred to above. The professional controversies as to the *limits* of the truth or usefulness of concepts should not mislead us, however. The two concepts or sets of concepts we are dealing with here are not necessarily antithetical, but rather are customarily supplementary over a large area of social analysis.

As structural-functional analysis provides tools for dealing with recurrent phenomena, the concept of culture provides tools for dealing with *variety*. The feeling or intuition that administration is administration wherever it is comes very quickly to the student of administration; and this theme is heavily emphasized in the American literature dealing with administration. Yet the student will also become aware, as he advances, that there are important *differences* between administrative systems, depending upon the location, the tasks, the environment, and the inhabitants of the system. And he needs handles by which he can grasp and deal with the differences.

Our present concern is with the differences between private and public administration. The thesis here is that unless we take the broad view provided by intercultural comparison, we are likely to fall into error, designating a distinction as universal when it is a true or important distinction only in our own country or cultural tradition. There come to mind here the common generalizations of writers in the United States which are true of a significant part or aspect of public administration in liberal democratic societies, but are by no means true of public administration by definition, as is implied or suggested. Precisely, consider the generalization that public administration is distinguished by special care for equality of treatment, legal authorization of and responsibility for action, public justification or justifiability of decisions, financial probity and meticulousness, and so forth. It does not take much knowledge of comparative administration to appreciate the very limited applicability of these characteristics to some "public" administration.

The concept of culture—plus knowledge about the actual culture—enables us to see administration in any particular society in relation to all factors which surround and condition it: political theories, educational system, class and caste distinctions, economic technology, and so forth. And enabling us to see administration in terms of its environment, it enables us to understand differences in administration between different societies which would be inexplicable if we were limited to viewing administration analytically in terms of the universals of administration itself. *For as the constituent parts of culture vary within a society, or between societies, so does administration vary as a system of rational cooperative action in that society, or between societies.* Administration is a part of the cultural complex; and it not only is acted upon, it acts. Indeed, by definition a system of rational cooperative action, it inaugurates and controls much change. Administration may be thought of as the major invention and device by which civilized men in complex societies try to control their culture, by which they seek simultaneously to achieve—within the limitations of their wit and knowledge—the goals of stability and the goals of change.

What Is Public Administration? A Summary Explanation

Let us return again to the question: What is *public* administration? The ideas associated with structural-functional analysis and culture will not enable us to *define* public with precision, but they help us in understanding the significance and implications of the term. They help us to understand why public administration has some general or generic aspects but also why the line between public and private is drawn in different places and with differing results—why "public" doesn't have precisely the same meaning in any two different cultural contexts. They help make some sense of the undoubted facts of similarity in diversity and diversity in similarity that characterize the Universe of Administration.

Whether public administration is an art or a science depends upon the meaning and emphasis one assigns these terms. The answer is affected too by the kind of public administration referred to—the study or discipline on the one hand, the activity or process on the other.

The central idea of public administration is rational action, defined as action correctly calculated to realize given desired goals. Public administration both as a *study* and as an *activity* is intended to maximize the realization of goals; and often the two blend into each other, since in the last analysis study is also a form of action.

Administration is cooperative human action with a high degree of rationality. Human action is *cooperative* if it has effects that would be absent if the cooperation did not take place. The significance of *high degree* of rationality lies in the fact that human cooperation varies in effectiveness of goal attainment, whether we think in terms of formal goals, the goals of leaders, or the goals of all who cooperate.

The distinguishing characteristics of an administrative system, seen in the customary perspective of administrative students, are best subsumed under two concepts, organization and management, thought of as analogous to anatomy and physiology in a biological system. *Organization* is the structure of authoritative *and* habitual personal interrelations in an administrative system. *Management* is action intended to achieve rational cooperation in an administrative system.

The significance of *public* can be sought in varying ways, each having some utility. For some purposes, for example, a simple determination of the legal status of an administrative system will suffice. For some important purposes, however, it is desirable to go beyond the boundaries of public administration as it has conventionally been studied and to adopt some of the concepts and tools of sociology and anthropology. *Structural-functional analysis* helps to identify the generic meaning or enduring significance of *public* in all societies. The concept of culture, on the other hand, helps in identifying and dealing with the varying aspects of *public* between societies, as well as with various relations of administration within a society.

The Importance of Nonrational Action

In this attempt to define and explain public administration in brief compass we have constructed a simple model. Of necessity many concepts of importance in the study of public administration have been omitted, and some of the concepts included have been dealt with rather summarily. Some of the omitted concepts are introduced, and perhaps some of the inadequacies repaired, in the following chapters. This is the appropriate place, however, to deal with what is perhaps a bias or distortion in our model, since the basis or source of the distortion largely lies outside of the later discussions.

The point is this: perhaps the model, by stressing rational action, creates a false impression of the amount of rationality (as defined) existing or possible in human affairs.

Now we may properly hold that the concept of rational action is placed at the center of administrative study and action. This is what it is about, so to speak. But the emphasis needs to be qualified—mellowed—by knowledge and appreciation of the nonrational. It is now generally agreed that earlier students of administration had a rationalist bias that led them to overestimate the potentialities of man (at least in the foreseeable future) for rational action.

Most of the streams of modern psychology emphasize—indeed perhaps overemphasize—the irrational component in human psychology: the role of the conditioned response, the emotive, the subconscious. Much of anthropology and sociology stresses complementary themes: the large amount of adaptive social behavior that is below the level of individual—and even group—conscious choice of goals and means to realize the goals. (The fact that goals are not chosen consciously does not mean that there are no goals in this behavior, nor that the goals are necessarily unimportant, nor even that they are any less true or meaningful than those consciously chosen. A baby responding to food stimuli, for example, is not choosing the goal of survival—but survival is usually thought a highly important goal. Actually, though such words as *conscious* and *unconscious* or *deliberate* and *adaptive* suggest two different realms of behavior, there is probably no sharp break, but rather varying levels of awareness of ends and means.)

The general picture that the nonrationalist conclusion of the psychologists, anthropologists, and sociologists (and others—the sources and manifestations of this mode of thought are many) present for the student of administration is this: An administrative organization has an internal environment and an external environment that are largely nonrational, at least so far as the formal goals of the administrative organization are concerned. People do not come into administrative organizations as pieces of putty, as units of abstract energy, nor as mere tools sharpened to some technical or professional purpose. They bring with them their whole cultural conditioning and their personal idiosyncrasies. Each is genetically unique, and all are members of institutions—families, churches, clubs, unions, and so forth—outside the administrative organization; and within the administrative organization they form into natural or adaptive groups of various kinds—friendships, cliques, car pools, and so forth—that flow across the lines of formal administrative organization, sometimes darkening, sometimes lightening, and sometimes erasing these lines.

Students of administration have become increasingly aware of the nonrational factors that surround and condition administration. They have broadened the base of their study to include much information that was formerly either unavailable or ignored. The goal of rationality has not been abandoned. Rather, it has been put in a new perspective: to achieve rationality demands a respect for the large area of the nonrational and much knowledge of it. Partly this new perspective is but a more serious heeding of Bacon's maxim: "Nature to be commanded must be obeyed." (These nonrational factors are not to be understood as, by definition, working against formal organization goals, but rather, paradoxically, as phenomena which, properly understood, can often be directed toward the realization of organization goals. They are resources as well as liabilities. Thus personal rivalries can be channeled—as by an official contest—to help rather than hinder goal achievement.) Partly the new perspective is a philosophical or psychological reorientation, as implied in the word *respect*. Students of administration now know that they are not going to take heaven by storm, that is to say, quickly reduce human affairs to rule and chart. Some of them, even, without ceasing to desire and strive for more rationality than we have now achieved, are heard to say that complete rationality in human affairs is not the proper goal; that a world in which *all* is orderly and predictable, with no room for spontaneity, surprise, and emotional play, is an undesirable world.

Footnotes to Chapter One. What Is Public Administration?

1. Another distinction, related and similar to the distinction between science and art, is that between pure and applied, or theoretical and practical, science. This distinction, which has important uses, is discussed below in connection

with logical positivism. For a statement of it see Herbert A. Simon: *Administrative Behavior: A Study of Decision-Making Processes in Administrative Organization* (New York, The Macmillan Co., 1947), Appendix.

2. This is an important—and difficult—word. One source of difficulty lies in the fact that given actions may produce desired results for the wrong reasons. Thus actions enjoined by superstition are found sometimes to be correct (i.e. goal-maximizing) by science, but the explanations in the two systems of interpretation are quite different. Another source of difficulty or ambiguity is discussed under The Meaning of Management.

3. See *Politics, Economics and Welfare* (New York, Harper & Brothers, 1953) by Robert A. Dahl and Charles E. Lindblom for a discussion of different forms of rational cooperation.

4. Sometimes a distinction is made between *purpose* and *function* in an attempt to deal with this problem. Dahl and Lindblom (p. 38) apply the idea of *net* goal achievement to the problem of multiple goals. "What do we mean by 'rationality'? And how can one test whether one action is more rational than another? The first question is easier to answer than the second. An action is rational to the extent that it is 'correctly' designed to maximize goal achievement, given the goal in question and the real world as it exists. Given more than one goal (the usual human situation), an action is rational to the extent that it is correctly designed to maximize *net* goal achievement."

5. This analogy is for introductory and explanatory purposes, and is to be viewed in this light. The definitions of organization and management that follow in the text admittedly comprehend less than the whole of societal anatomy and physiology respectively. And we are not here concerned with the familiar sociological distinction between patterns and consequences, or with distinguishing between static and dynamic models.

chapter two

Development of the Study of Administration

Administration has been studied since the dawn of history, but seldom with much self-consciousness, and never before with the scope and intensity of today.

Historical Roots of Administration

A fascinating sketch of the development of administration in the dawn of history is presented in V. Gordon Childe's chapter "The Urban Revolution in Mesopotamia" in his *What Happened in History* (New York, Penguin Books, Inc., 1946). The nucleus of the Sumerian cities and civilization was the divine household, which began as an enlarged version of the patriarchal household of barbarism. These divine households were "administered" by corporations of priests and were centered in temples which were not merely places of worship but centers of industry and agriculture. They contained stores of foodstuffs which were technically, as was nearly everything, the property of the gods. Agriculture was generally supervised from the temple: canal building, allotment of land and produce, breeding and seeding. Within the temples too crafts such as those of textile-making and metal-working became differentiated and specialized.

To fulfill the needs of administration, writing and various forms of measurement and mathematics were invented. Written record—extended and permanent memory—was a necessity to any high degree of rationality; temple accounts had to be intelligible to their user, to colleagues and successors. Moreover, without them how could accountability to the gods be enforced? Measurements of weight, space, and time were needed in agriculture and industry and were forthcoming (one of them, the twenty-four-hour day, survives). Simple forms of arithmetic and geometry were devised, and astral observations were systematized and made useful as an aid to agriculture. A "commodity to measure commodities" was needed and was found in conventionalized pieces of precious metals; the transition from a natural to a money economy took place.

Now the ancient Sumerians no doubt would have been surprised to be told they were learning to administer (nor does Childe use this word in the account summarized above). In their own eyes they were simply solving practical problems, and probably even many discoveries of a "better way" were accidental. But they were nevertheless learning to administer. They would also have been surprised to learn that they were developing physical science, but just as clearly they were doing so.

This simple ancient setting reveals, incidentally, the close interdependence of social and physical science. We cannot read this record without being impressed with the fact that the social inventions either preceded or were concomitant with the physical, and that without the social, the physical would not have occurred. May we not then set forth for reflection and study a thesis: that the conventional distinction between physical and social science[1] is unrealistic, that any extended development in one inevitably entails development in the other? Or put another way, that there are not two processes here, but essentially one. To go back to the introductory example, is the releasing of nuclear energy conceivable without a preceding multitude of social inventions—including one of the greatest social inventions, the "invention of invention" itself?

The history of administration, as such, remains for the most part unwritten, though in Western civilization its main outlines are clear. Historians have customarily written history from some other perspective than that of the student of administration: as the lives of great men, as the stories of nations, as the influence of economics, and so forth. Incidental to their main preoccupations, however, the historians have thrown some light on the main administrative developments. And a few, especially in recent years, have addressed themselves directly and in detail to administration in a particular time and setting. The administrative history of England, for example, has been given very intensive study in some periods and aspects. In the United States a professional student of administration, Leonard D. White, has turned to history and published two important studies of our early national administration.[2]

Administration has been studied in every age and at every stage of history, but with great variation in means, intensity, and awareness. Much of the study has been within a particular administrative system: persons have gone to work in administration, learned their jobs, and perhaps according to ability and circumstances sought more or less consciously to find better ways of administering—which better ways in turn might be learned by others. History records also much study in preparation for participation in administration. Most frequently this study in preparation has been legal learning of some kind. There are various reasons for this. One is that the laws being studied were actually those that were to govern administration or to be administered. Another is the fact that training in law develops attitudes and habits of mind useful in administration, at least at a certain level of its development: familiarity with abstract and logical thinking, ability to categorize and generalize, respect for rules, training in relating rules to facts in the making of decisions.

Of course nearly anything learned at home or in school can later be put to use in an administrative system; and it is an important fact of history that nearly all of the founding and supporting of institutions of learning in the medieval and early modern periods was carried out for precisely this reason: by Church or State for the training of people for more effective performance in an administration system. Much general education and specialized training still is aimed at this avowed purpose. And though in America we think of education primarily in terms of enabling individuals to better themselves in some way, nevertheless the *result* or *function* of education is in large part the preparation of persons for effective participation in an administrative system. Consider, for example, the engineer who makes his career with an industrial firm or a city government, or the accountant who finds his employment either in private industry or civil service. How many people today are self-employed and work alone?

Development of the Study of Administration

In the late nineteenth and early twentieth centuries important developments took place in the study of administration. These developments have tremendously changed the perspective, the scope, and the content of administrative study, so much that it is no exaggeration to say that collectively they constitute a revolution or mutation in human culture. What has occurred, in essence, is a great increase in man's ability to achieve goals through cooperative action—goals good and bad. Much of this increase has already occurred, much more is in prospect.

It is not easy in short space to describe and characterize what has happened. For that matter, it would not be easy to describe and characterize what has happened at great length, for the story is very complicated, is still but dimly understood, and is yet to be studied as history. Searching for a summary or characterization, we can do no better than say that for the first time man arrived at a full awareness of administration as a process and problem, in general and in the abstract.[3] For the first time he was able to view the process and the problem of its improvement completely from the outside, and had the time, interest, and inclination for sustained attention to it.

Man arrived at this condition as the result of the convergence of a great number and variety of historical trends. One was the upward trend in the study and effectiveness of administration itself. Administrative systems gradually become larger and more complex in modern history, and while size and complexity are not necessarily true measures of cooperative effectiveness and rationality in particular cases, nevertheless they are crude indexes of the growth of knowledge of how to achieve human goals—at least the goals that modern Western man has sought. The proof is in the results, the massive changes in the physical aspects of life on earth (unless one wishes to make the implausible assertion that these changes have taken place *despite* the increase in size and complexity of administrative systems).

Modern Physical Science and Technology

Another great historical trend underlying the administrative revolution[4] was of course the spectacular development of modern physical science and technology. This oft-told tale need not be repeated. It is enough to recall that the nineteenth century witnessed a spectacular growth of the iron-coal-steam technology, a flood of new inventions and discoveries, a never-ending proliferation of new sciences and technologies. According to the thesis put forth above, the distinction between social and physical science is a false one; and force is given the thesis by the simultaneous development of administrative effectiveness and physical technology. Telephones, for example, permit an increase in the size and effectiveness of administrative systems; but telephones cannot be made, installed, and operated without large and complex administrative systems. These systems no more just happened than did the telephone.

The intellectual elegance and empirical utility of mathematical and conceptual systems such as Newtonian mechanics inspired attempts from the seventeenth century onward to duplicate such feats for the social realm. The results have been mixed. Much nonsense and worse has been perpetrated in the name of science by transposing concepts and techniques from realms where they are appropriate and useful to realms where they are not. On the other hand, much useful transposing and adaptation have been brought about. In any case, the achievements of modern science and technology have served as a continual spur to effort in social science and technology. This spur and the belief that the methods of physical science can and should be transferred to social phenomena lie back of the reorientation of administrative study in the nineteenth and twentieth centuries.

The Scientific Management Movement

One of the main chapters and perhaps the central themes in the story concerns the Scientific Management movement. This movement is associated prominently, though by no means exclusively, with the name of Frederick W. Taylor. Taylor was a foreman and manager in a Pennsylvania steel company in the eighteen-nineties and early years of the present century. Having a scientific bent of mind, he performed very elaborate experiments in steel-cutting methods, with results of high utility; personal, empirical, hit-and-miss steel-cutting methods were replaced by a One Best Way.

Taylor's intellectual curiosity then led him to experiment with human operations in steel production to determine whether they too lent themselves to the discovery of a One Best Way. He put himself to work isolating and measuring all possible variables in his men, their tools, and their methods. His conclusions were positive. The results of his experiments demonstrated conclusively (to him) that there are scientifically ascertainable and demonstrable best ways to perform muscular work such as shoveling. Thus the door to important developments was opened a tiny crack. If there is a scientifically ascertainable way of determining the One Best Way to load iron pigs, might not the same methods, at least if sharpened and improved, serve to discover the One Best Way to perform complex human operations? Might not the dream of making social science really scientific at last come true?

Taylor, joined by others (some would say preceded by others), pursued this dream. One manufacturing and commercial operation after another was subjected to study in the new method and spirit, with the usual conclusion that more effective—more efficient and economical—methods had been discovered. The method and spirit, now named *Scientific Management*, spread beyond industry and commerce to group enterprises generally, including those of public administration. The movement spread abroad (even Lenin, the chief founder of Russian Communism, spoke favorably of Taylorism) and an international scientific-management society was set up. This society still exists, but the original fervor has faded, the original methods have been superseded. To understand what has happened, however, Taylorism must be envisaged not as a solitary mountain in a plain, but as a dominating peak in a range atop a plateau. Taylorism was a thrust upward toward better, more rational, and more effective methods of administration at a very high point. While Taylorism has all but lost its separate identity, its effects were felt, and still are felt, in nearly all areas of administrative study.[5]

Basic Transformations in American Society

The first general textbooks on public administration, published in the United States in the mid-twenties, acknowledge their indebtedness to the Scientific Management movement. Law as the chief basis for administrative study and action is explicitly abandoned for the management outlook. But many other events, influences, and currents of thought are also reflected in these textbooks. It is beyond the scope of this essay to discuss them fully, but some of these other contributing factors can at least be identified.

Among events there were, for example, the closing of the frontier, conventionally dated at 1890, and the transition of American society from a predominantly agricultural and rural to a predominantly industrial and urban condition, which took place between 1900 and 1910. Together these two events presented a new problem of government. The Jeffersonian and Jacksonian interpretation of the meaning of democracy, which were widely accepted and well-adapted to the conditions of American life in the early nineteenth century, became more and more questionable as the economy became more complicated and the complex problems of city living presented themselves. The Jeffersonian-Jacksonian philosophy of democracy was one which tended toward suspicion of government per se, which favored individual action over group action, and favored amateurism and frequent changes in office (by the fortunes of politics or the spoils system, as it worked out). As the country moved rapidly into an industrial-urban condition following the Civil War, our inherited ideas and institutions proved so inadequate that appalling conditions of inefficiency, dishonesty, and chaos resulted. Many sensitive and patriotic citizens became alarmed for the continued existence of our republican institutions.

New Theories of Government

The rise of public administration as a self-conscious study is undoubtedly a response to this situation. It is an attempt to make government work under the new and more demanding conditions, by increasing the amount of systematic study of the problems of government and the competence and training of those entering government service. Public administration as a literature and a body of concepts also came to contain a new theory or philosophy of government. In essence, this new theory or philosophy of government was a reinterpretation of the meaning of democracy for America, one for the new, urban America. At the risk of oversimplification it can be said that the new philosophy of government sought the attainment of Jeffersonian ends by Hamiltonian means. It sought to attain the values of equality and freedom for citizens by making government strong and efficient, but simultaneously responsible and democratic. To attain these latter objectives, political reforms as well as administrative reforms were proposed as a part of a single program. Instead of dispersal of functions and powers in the Jeffersonian-Jacksonian fashion, functions and powers were to be closely concentrated, then professionally performed under close public scrutiny—which meant reforms like the short ballot.

Woodrow Wilson was prominent among those who fashioned the new theories; he was also a Founding Father of public administration as a discipline.[6] These new theories extended beyond the developing literature of public administration, though they centered there. They are accepted more or less by most Americans today, and have disappeared beneath the surface of the professional writings. But it usually does not take much probing beneath the surface to discover that they are still there.

Growth of the Field of Political Science

Developments of other kinds were reflected in the first textbooks. One of these was the growth of the field of political science as a separate and substantial area of academic research and teaching. While statecraft or political science, like administration, has been taught and learned in some fashion since the dawn of history, it grew greatly in scope and depth during the late nineteenth and early twentieth centuries in America; the present curriculum is hardly recognizable in germ in that of seventy-five years ago. Public administration as a discipline was brought to birth, or at least to self-consciousness, by political science. Woodrow Wilson, professor of politics and writer on public administration, has been cited. The authors of the first two textbooks, Leonard D. White and F. W. Willoughby,[7] were professors of political science; indeed all authors of subsequent textbooks have been academically trained political scientists. Meanwhile, however, public administration, though closely related to general political science, has gained a position of considerable autonomy. The American Society for Public Administration, consisting now of about 7,000 teachers, researchers, and practitioners of public administration, was formed in 1939 and exists independent of the American Political Science Association. Additionally there have grown up a host of other organizations of larger or smaller size and more or less specialized character—organizations of personnel workers, finance officers, city managers, social-welfare workers, prison administrators, and so forth.

Growth of Higher Education

Another development which lies behind and is reflected in the first textbooks is the growth of higher education. The university system, borrowing much from the German university, which was then at the pinnacle of its prestige, came to assume its present outlines. The serious attention to science and the provision for high specialization which characterize the American university have American roots, to be sure, but were forwarded by large numbers of educators who had studied at a continental university. The drive toward scientific and professional achievement thus implanted in the system of higher education has affected public administration. In point may be cited the case of William E. Mosher, one of the Founding Fathers who received his education in Germany. Mosher was largely responsible for the establishment of the Maxwell School of Citizenship and Public Affairs at Syracuse University, a leading center of administrative study and training; and he was coauthor of the first general textbook of personnel administration.

Public Administration Comes of Age: The Impact of Other Factors

Space does not permit a complete cataloguing of the factors responsible for the attainment by public administration of self-consciousness, as we may call it. But a few others can be noted. National emergencies have had a catalyzing effect, presenting challenges to which new thinking about and action in public administration were responses. The First World War inaugurated some developments and hastened others, such as the extension of Scientific Management thinking into government circles and the establishment of a Federal budget system, which took place in 1921. The Great Depression of the thirties and the Second World War have had similar forcing effects.

The emergence or growth of other new sciences and professions has shaped public administration in numerous ways. The burgeoning of modern scientific psychology in the past seventy-five years may be cited as an important example. While the Founding Fathers were not in this case an important channel of influence, such apparatuses and techniques of psychology as intelligence- and aptitude-testing were nevertheless adopted for use in personnel administration at an early date and have had a subtle, pervasive influence. In recent years there has been a conscious and extensive effort to adapt and use as much psychology as is adaptable and usable. In fact one of the recent textbooks of public administration takes social psychology as its matrix or perspective.[8]

Fashions in philosophy have also had their influence in the study of public administration. During the past two generations would-be tough-minded schools of philosophy (as their adherents like to think) have been popular among academic and scientific people; there has been a turning away from types of philosophy that stress the a priori, the transcendental, the ideal, and a turning toward types of philosophy that stress experience, the observable, reality in the physical sense. These tough-minded schools—materialism, empiricism, positivism, realism, and pragmatism are some of the schools or labels—have in common that they claim to be associated with modern physical science, to represent or interpret science.

The tough-minded philosophies have been popular among students of administration. This is easily understandable, given the general climate of opinion in which they worked and their ardent desire to make administration a science. One can even say, with the wisdom of hindsight, that it could hardly have been otherwise. Pragmatism, popularized by William James and especially John Dewey—a philosophy which stresses experience and action and makes usefulness the test of truth—has been influential (to judge from the evidence of words) with some students. Logical positivism, which stresses experience and verifiability but also stresses logic and semantic analysis, has been more recently in vogue. Logical positivism has provided for some contemporary writers logical (or perhaps psychological) foundations upon which substantive inquiries into administration could be built. Some of the issues raised by logical positivism in administrative study and action are discussed in Chapter Six.

This discussion of the development of administrative study has gradually become centered upon *public* administration. But in conclusion, our perspective should again be broadened.

At the same time that public administration was gaining self-consciousness, taking shape as a discipline and an academic curriculum, *business administration* was similarly gaining self-consciousness and taking shape as a discipline and curriculum. In many ways the two are similar. They have many identical or similar concepts and techniques; sometimes they are studied and taught together in the same school or department; both are species of the same genus.

It is to be noted, however, that the adjective *business* instead of *private* is used. Business administration tends to focus rather sharply upon organization and management in what we think of as the economic field; relationships of academic departments of business administration are on the whole probably closer with academic departments of economics than with departments of political science. This is not said in criticism, but merely to make the point that there is an area of administration which falls between public administration and business administration as these are currently studied and taught. This area might be identified as private and noneconomic (churches, for example, would be so classified, as well as most pressure groups) but it includes also some administrative systems or activities which are on the shadowy, fluctuating borderline between public and private administration. Probably this area deserves more attention than it now receives.

Footnotes to Chapter Two. Development of the Study of Administration

1. The word *science* here should be read in the light of the discussion in the first pages of Chapter One. *Physical technology* and *social technology* may be substituted.

2. Leonard D. White: *The Federalists: A Study in Administrative History* (New York, The Macmillan Co., 1948); and *The Jeffersonians: A Study in Administrative History, 1801–1829* (New York, The Macmillan Co., 1951).

3. What I call the attainment of self-consciousness is illustrated in the following quotation from the *Philosophy of Management* (London, Sir Isaac Pitman & Sons, 1924) by Oliver Sheldon. Sheldon, a Britisher, was at least in a loose sense a member of the international Scientific Management movement discussed in the text. This quotation appeared on the first page of the first textbook on public administration:

   "Management has gradually become a profession. Its task has increased in difficulty, responsibility, and complexity, until today it touches all sciences, from chemistry and mechanics to psychology and medicine. It calls to its service, therefore, men and women with tact and ideals, with the highest scientific qualifications and with a strong capacity for organization and leadership. It is employing lawyers and doctors, accountants and artists, and by directing their professions, is forming a supreme profession of its own, with all the implications consequent upon such a line of progress of standards, qualifications, apprenticeship, and technique."

4. A professional economist, K. E. Boulding, recently published a very interesting book titled *The Organizational Revolution: A Study in the Ethics of Economic Organization* (New York, Harper & Brothers, 1953). In Part I the author seeks the "nature, causes, and effects" of the great increase in the number, size, and complexity of organizations during the past century in Western society.

5. There is a voluminous and easily accessible literature dealing with Taylor and the Scientific Management movement. Taylor's book, *The Principles of Scientific Management*, first published in 1911 but available in later editions, should probably come first. It is a document interesting on its human as well as its scientific side.

6. Wilson's essay, "The Study of Administration," *Pol. Sci. Quart.* 2:197–222 (1887) is perhaps the most famous of American writings on public administration. It is reprinted in the author's book of readings, *Ideas and Issues in Public Administration* (New York, McGraw-Hill Book Company, Inc., 1953).

7. White, *Introduction to the Study of Public Administration* (New York, The Macmillan Co., 1926) and Willoughby, *Principles of Public Administration* (Washington, D.C., Brookings Institution, 1927). Professor White's book, now in its third edition, has been a standard work for a generation.

8. *Public Administration* (New York, Alfred A. Knopf, Inc., 1950) by Herbert A. Simon, Donald W. Smithburg, and Victor A. Thompson.

chapter three

Contemporary Teaching and Training

||||||||||||||||||||||||||||||||||||||||||||||||||||||||||||||||||||||||||||||||||||||||||||||||||||||||||||||||||||||||||||||||||||||||||||||||||||||

It is time now to take a look at the scope and content of present-day courses in public administration, and to survey the various ways in which public administration is taught and its practitioners formally trained.

Contents of Two Typical Basic Textbooks

There is no better way to begin than to review the tables of contents of two recently published general textbooks—identically titled *Public Administration*. Some of the chapter and topic titles will no doubt be puzzling to the beginner in public administration. Some will be clarified below, and, for the present, general impressions and comparisons are sufficient.

In colleges, universities, and training programs in which only one course in public administration is taught, this course is customarily built around one of the half-dozen or more general textbooks now available. If more than one course is taught, the general course built around one of the textbooks is often a prerequisite for the others.

The table of contents for the first book contains chapter titles only; for the second, topical headings as well. Despite the appearance of greater length thus conveyed, the second book is actually slightly shorter than the first.

CONTENTS*

Part I

Public Administration in the Modern State

1. What Is Public Administration?
2. Why Big Government?
3. The Nature and Role of Bureaucracy

Part II

The Dynamics of Administration

4. Executive Leadership
5. Administrative Planning

---

* From *Public Administration* (3rd ed., 1953) by John M. Pfiffner and R. Vance Presthus. Copyrighted by and reproduced by permission of The Ronald Press Company. (Page numbers omitted.)

CONTENTS*

---

* From *Public Administration* (1953) by M. E. Dimock and G. O. Dimock.
Reproduced by permission of Rinehart & Company, Inc. Abridged by omission
of case studies, summaries, and page numbers.

Forms of Organization
Characteristic Strengths and Weaknesses
Special Problems of Governmental Organization
Departmental Organization
The Independent Regulatory Commission
Government Corporations
On Government Reorganization in General
VI. Personnel
Principal Steps in Personnel Administration
Landmarks in the Evolution of Personnel Administration
The Proper Division of Functions in a Personnel System
Problems of Personnel Administration
The Problem of Neutrality
The Guild Spirit in Administration
Employee Loyalty and National Security
Corruption in Government Employment
The Uses and Misuses of Position Classification
Commission versus a Single Personnel Administrator
Leadership at the Top
Government Service as a Career
Internship Programs
Retirement Systems
VII. Finance
Why Financial Administration Is Important
How Financial Administration Determines Policy
The Framework of Financial Administration
At the Top Level
At the Operating Level
Budget Administration
Budgeting in the States
Budget Bureau and Legislative Action on the Budget
The Need for a Performance Budget
Where Should the Budget Function Be Located?
Accounting and Auditing
Proposals for Accounting Reform
Progress under the Hoover Commission and Joint Program
Purchasing and Supply

Part III

Getting the Job Done

VIII. Leadership
Why Demands on Leadership Have Changed
The Role of Authority in Administration
Winning Acceptance for Organization Goals
Steps in Executive Leadership
Job Analysis
Administrative Delegation of Authority

Part IV

Democratic Control

Fundamental Similarities between the Books

It is apparent to anyone who reads these tables of contents thoughtfully that there is a general similarity in content and in the pattern of treatment, despite obvious differences of approach and style of treatment. Both begin with an attempt to orient the student, to impress upon him the scope and importance of public administration and the need for study and training. Both then proceed to discuss dynamics, the first of administration, the second of policy formation. There is a difference in emphasis here, but not as great as the wording of the tables suggests.

Both books then proceed to discuss the structure and the functioning of administration. Both discuss organization, personnel, and finance, in the same order. The second book seems to stress somewhat more the techniques of administration, and probably does so in fact, but again not to the extent suggested by the wording of the tables (much of its Part III, Getting the Job Done, is contained in other chapters of the first book).

Both books then proceed to discuss the legal content and aspects of public administration, the first book having the greater emphasis here. Both books end on the same theme, the problem of how to make public administration responsible, how to keep it under control.

How Both Books Differ from Early Texts

Both books differ from the earliest textbooks in administration more significantly than they differ from each other, so swift has been the pace of developments in administrative study and practice. Neither emphasizes as strongly the structural aspects of administration; neither is as certain that there are known, fixed principles of administration of the same nature as those in the physical sciences; neither treats as fully (or as self-confidently) certain staff or housekeeping functions. Both pay considerably more attention to the political setting of public administration than the first texts; both pay more attention to policy formulation and execution; both utilize many data from psychological study and other social sciences that were not even available a quarter-century ago; both have a flexibility and sophistication which could not possibly have characterized the pioneering efforts.

Comparison of Two Other Recent Textbooks

Two other recent textbooks deserve our attention. One of these is *Public Administration* (New York, Alfred A. Knopf, Inc., 1950) by Herbert A. Simon, Donald W. Smithburg, and Victor A. Thompson. This book follows many of the familiar patterns. It begins with a chapter titled "What Is Public Administration?" and ends with two chapters on administrative responsibility. Yet it stands apart as different in flavor and content from the other half-dozen available textbooks. In what does this difference consist?

It consists, first of all, in a conscious and rather rigorous commitment to some of the principles of logical-positivist philosophy. The meaning of this will be examined at least briefly below; here attention is focused on the book. The result in terms of the book is that there is an attempt to minimize or avoid all "ought" matters.[1] Not only is there an attempt to avoid stating what government should do, in general or in the United States in particular, but there is an attempt to avoid what the authors regard as "excessive preoccupation with 'ideal' or 'desirable' administrative arrangements."[2] There is deep determination to be scientific, as the authors conceive it, to avoid completely the field of ethics.[3]

Second, this textbook goes further than any other in bringing in concepts and data from the disciplines of psychology, sociology, and some of the other fields of inquiry concerned with human behavior in nonadministrative contexts or in general. Its authors try both to supplement and to correct, to substitute "fact for fancy in the theory of administration."

Third, there is less attention to some of the legal and factual aspects of American administration than is customary.[4] This characteristic is perhaps a necessary corollary of the second, given a book of a certain length. In terms of an example, this textbook has a very penetrating discussion of staff theory and psychology, but less material than is customary on the history, organization, and operation of the staff facilities of the President.

The other textbook is *Management in the Public Service: The Quest for Effective Performance* (New York, McGraw-Hill Book Company, Inc., 1954) by John D. Millett. The focus of this textbook is narrower than that of the conventional type. This is true largely because the author has planned the book as one of two companion volumes, the other not yet written. The companion volume is to deal with the "politics of administration," that is to say, with the setting of administration in terms of legal norms, political processes, and perhaps policy development.

The focus in this volume is on management, with some emphasis upon the problems of the chief manager, but with an attempt to find the common denominators of management problems. "The word 'management' in the title here implies that our interest is in the operation of administrative agencies as such. The apex of our attention for the present is the department head or the chief officer of any other separate administrative agency of government. Moreover, as already suggested, this volume deals with the *common* problems of management, with the interests and concerns of management which spread from one agency to another regardless of its substantive field of activity."[5] The three parts of the book are labeled as follows: The Common Problems of Work Direction, The Common Problems of Work Operation, and The Common Problems of Internal Services.

Perhaps it should be added that though the focus is on management, organization is not neglected, but treated as a problem in management; and that the volume reflects also the increasing acclimatization of concepts and data of the various social sciences in administrative study.

Patterns of Course Organization

In colleges and universities in which more than a single general course in public administration is taught, the other courses are most likely to be specialized along one or the other or both of two lines. One type of specialization is geographical and legal: courses on national, state, municipal, local, and international administration. The other line of specialization is functional, following subject-matter or activity patterns within administration: courses on personnel administration, budgeting or financial administration, planning, administrative law, and so forth.

One of the important recent trends in study and teaching of public administration, as suggested above, has been to relate the core of organization and management to functions and policy—actual areas of government activity such as agriculture, forestry, and social services. (This trend reverses an earlier drive towards autonomy, a desire to achieve a study or discipline of administration "in itself," which was a natural aspect of what I have called the achievement of self-consciousness. The discipline, having successfully asserted itself as a focus of interest, needs no longer to be so jealous about its purity.) One way this trend has been reflected is in an increase of courses on public policy, such as courses on government regulation of business. Much of the bringing together of public administration and public policy (the how and the what) comes from the other direction: many students in professional schools and specialized subject-matter curricula are encouraged or required to pass at least a general course in public administration to develop competence in, or at least awareness of, the formal cooperative aspects of their profession or specialization. Many will be publicly employed, and some will become public administrators primarily, rather than practitioners of their original profession or specialty. Substantially all of the remainder will be dealing with public administration in some aspect of their profession or specialization.

Large teaching programs in public administration may contain still other types of courses, reflecting such factors as special institutional needs, fashionable trends in interest, or research specialties of the staff. Courses in the techniques of organizational analysis and management surveying are rather frequently found. Courses in official English (report-writing, etc.), lately expanded in concept and coverage to deal with the general problem of communication in the administrative context, are sometimes given. Lately, growing out of our broadened world-view, an interest in comparative and international administration has found expression in some curricula.

Usually public administration is taught as a part of the broader curriculum, political science, an arrangement which reflects both the historical lineage of public administration and its public orientation. In some institutions the public-administration curriculum has assumed separate status as a program or school. In either case the teaching relationship with political science is almost certainly regarded as important, and the student is expected or required to round out his preparation for study or practice by addressing himself to the study of various aspects of general political theory, American governmental institutions, international relations and agencies, comparative government and politics, public law and jurisprudence, and parties, politics, and pressure groups.

Political science in turn is not taught in isolation, and beyond the complex of facts, interests, and courses customarily regarded as political science are the other social sciences—for that matter, the range of liberal arts and physical science which constitute present higher education in America. (Some study of languages, literature, mathematics, and physical science is a degree requirement prior to or contemporaneous with special study of public administration.) The student of public administration is encouraged or required within the limits of his time and energy to supplement his courses in public administration by study not only of political science but also in disciplines such as history, sociology, economics, social psychology, business administration, and anthropology. Some tool subjects regarded as of especial value in achieving rational cooperative action are often required; most frequent are statistics and accounting. While few, whether students or practitioners, need become skilled producers, many or all need to be intelligent consumers of the common techniques of quantification. Indeed, quantification is one of the surest means—some would say the only adequate test—of rational action (as defined above).

An Actual Program: Cornell University

Substance will be given these generalizations about curriculum by a look at an actual program of study. At hand is the *Announcement for Sessions of 1954–55* of the School of Business and Public Administration at Cornell University. This School is for graduate study, specifically "to train men and women for professional careers in private business and the public service"; as the name indicates, it is built upon the theory that business and public administration are closely related and should be brought under one roof for educational purposes. The *Announcement* emphasizes that not only are business and public administration under one roof, but instruction is carried on with "integrated combination" of the two.

The program is built upon three other principles, according to the statement of "Aim and Philosophy." One is the tenet that there are "universals of the administrative process" which are found in all large scale enterprises "whether they are public, private, educational, or military." The second

principle, however, is that the general concern of public-administration pro·
grams with the training of "administrative generalists" needs "substantial
supplementing, for it is clear that the ranks of management in both government and business include a very large number of men and women who
were originally trained as lawyers, educators, scientists, engineers, or professional people in any one of a great many fields." The program aims at
"supplementary" instruction for "those whose primary training may be in
any one of the technical and professional fields." The third principle is that
the student of administration must not only be trained in the universals of
the management process but also "receive instruction concerning the in-
strumental techniques of control for the improvement of decision-making
and policy formulation." To this end each student is expected to develop
a "more specialized body of knowledge in a selected field of concentration."

As to prerequisites the catalog states that predominant weight is given to
the quality of an applicant's record rather than particular courses.

It is recommended, however, that students who plan to enter the School
include in their undergraduate programs basic courses in economics, accounting,
statistics, and American government. Students who intend to specialize in
Public Administration should include courses in political science in their undergraduate programs prior to entering the School.

Most of the instruction of the School centers upon programs for the
master's degree. At the master's level, two professional degrees are conferred,
Master of Business Administration and Master of Public Administration.
The course of study for either degree is two years. The program for the first
year (except for one course not shown) is the same for both degrees, the
so-called core courses, as follows: Introduction to Administration, Administrative Accounting, Managerial Economics, Finance, and Statistics.

In the second year candidates for both degrees are required to take Business Policy and Economic Instability, and either Competitive Behavior and
Public Policy or National Administration and Public Policy.

In the second year students must also, however, "complete the require-
ments of a *concentration* plus approved elective hours sufficient to fill out
the minimum of 60 semester hours required for graduation."

The wording of the catalog concerning the Master of Public Administration program illustrates several points and lists the fields of concentration:

The M.P.A. Degree . . . The School's program in Public Administration
is based upon the central role of government in modern life, the rise of the
career public service, and the consequent increasing demand for trained public
managers. Recognizing the fact that public administration both assumes substantive policy-making responsibilities and also undertakes primary responsibility
for the processes of management, this School makes every effort to develop both
the student's knowledge and competence in administration and his knowledge
and understanding of public policy itself. While providing for a considerable
amount of individual concentration, the program is nevertheless primarily concerned with the development of public administrators who are at home both

with program problems and with the practicalities of day-to-day administrative activities.

The program is intended for students who aspire to careers in local, state, federal, or international agencies. It may also be designed for those who plan to work with private enterprise in the management of its relationships with government. Concentrations may be arranged in any one of these areas.

In view of the fact that the public service draws upon many professions, including law, engineering, accounting, public health, public welfare, agriculture, penology, and medicine, it is expected that students will come to the School with varying degrees of preparation and background in government and its administration. Because candidates from all these fields, as well as those with more general training, are encouraged to enroll, a particular effort is made to devise individual programs for each of the students. Since the School's enrollment is intentionally limited, it is possible to provide this specialized attention.

Concentrations for the Master of Public Administration degree are available in the fields of *agricultural management, city management, federal administration, international administration, public finance administration, public personnel management, transportation, and special.* [Italics in original.]

One example of a "concentration," that for the Master of Public Administration in Federal Administration, must suffice for this brief summary. A student preparing for this concentration "will elect second-year work with the approval of his adviser from among the following courses: Business Policy and Economic Instability, Seminar in Public Personnel Administration, National Administration and Public Policy, Problems in Public Administration, Seminar in Federal Administration, Management of Public Business Enterprises, Management Surveys—Organization and Methods, Governmental Fiscal Management, Transportation, The American Presidency, Taxation, and Federal Public Finance."

The Case Method of Teaching and Training

One recent development of considerable importance in teaching and training concerns cases and the case method. This development arose out of a feeling of dissatisfaction with the textbook approach to teaching and training. The dissatisfaction was both substantive and procedural. Substantively, there was a rather widespread feeling that the textbooks (those available several years ago, at least) set forth "facts" and "principles" which were not as firmly established as they were represented to be. Procedurally, there was a conviction that the vital juices of administrative life were squeezed out between the covers of a textbook, and that some way to make the student acquainted with administrative reality must be found.

The result was a sustained effort to develop some cases which should be presentations of actual administration in the round—literary or historical reconstructions from the written record and the memory of participants in real administrative events significant because of the problems and activities they exhibit. These cases would, it was thought, present public administration free from the possibly warping or erroneous preconceptions of the textbooks, and give the student a sense of what public administration is in fact like—so far as one can be made to sense it vicariously from the printed record. Recently, a large volume of cases, edited by Harold Stein and titled *Cases in Public Administration and Policy Formulation*,[6] was published and is being used experimentally from coast to coast. The cases concern various levels of jurisdiction (though chiefly the Federal), various levels of operation (though with some emphasis upon "front office"), and various types of functions or programs. Typical titles are: Transfer of the Children's Bureau, The Glavis-Ballinger Dispute, The Battle of Blue Earth County, The Disposal of the Aluminum Plants, The Air Search and Rescue Program, The FBI Retirement Bill, and The Attack on the Cost of Living Index. The cases are literary in quality, and many are fascinating narratives, with the photographic quality one associates with some contemporary short stories.

These cases are open-ended in the sense that they are not intended to prove but to illustrate, to suggest, to illumine—and indeed, to educate the emotions. As the editor says in his introduction, "This is a collection of cases that offers an incorrigible resistance to any highly systematic categorization."[7]

The tentative and experimental nature of the venture is both recognized and emphasized. It is clear, for example, that cases in the study of public administration are not closely analogous to cases in the study of law: established categories are not illumined by authoritative statements. There is a widespread feeling, however, that the case method is applicable, perhaps in various ways, in the development of administrative study. Incidentally, as indicated by the title, the volume under discussion illustrates another trend commented on above, namely, emphasizing questions of public policy and the decision-making process.[8]

In-Service Training

In this brief sketch of teaching and training for public administration there remains only to take note of in-service training. This expression as here used embraces all instruction or training that seeks to bridge the gap between regular, formal instruction and learning by actual administrative experience (though the term is usually restricted in meaning to some one type of such training).

One general type of such training is *pre-entry* training, similar to the apprenticeship or medical internship. It seeks in varying ways to give an experience of on-the-job conditions to one who is still engaged in, or just finished with, a program of formal instruction. A program may, for example, involve rapid rotation of students, singly or in groups, through several levels or agencies of a governmental jurisdiction (with its consent and cooperation, of course). During this rotation program the students perform simple administrative functions at every station in the rotation program and/or are taken in hand by a permanent member of the organization for instruction in the functions and expertise peculiar to that station. Or a program may involve for a student a year of intensive internship in a single position. Obviously, many types of programs are possible, and a great many types have been or are now being used. Some institutions emphasize this aspect of their program and feel that the results, as measured in the accomplishments of their students, abundantly prove its practicality.

The other general type of in-service training is *on-the-job* training. As a type it is the reverse of pre-entry training: it consists of more or less formal instruction for those already entered upon regular administrative employment and receiving remuneration. (Since interns sometimes receive regular compensation—and for other reasons—there is no sharp distinction between the two general types.)

As with pre-entry training so with on-the-job training, there is wide variety in the types of program possible. At what may be called one end of the scale, promising junior executives may be sent off for a sabbatical year of special study; or some special training course for all executives of a given age or with a given function may be given. At the other end of the scale are programs by which foremen instruct their workmen how to use tools or machinery or to cooperate effectively on a particular type of operation. Incidentally, such training programs have proved very efficacious, and the foreman's function is now conceived more as that of a teacher and less as that of a boss.

Footnotes to Chapter Three. Contemporary Teaching and Training

1. "The position has been taken in these pages that knowledge of administration, like all knowledge, is amoral. It becomes 'good' or 'bad' only in terms of the value assumptions added to it by the person who uses it—in terms of his attitudes towards goals and methods." Simon *et al., Op. cit.,* 22.

2. *Op. cit.,* ix.

3. "The study of the behavior of persons in organizations can be non-normative —that is, it can be freed from the desires, values, and prejudices of the person making the investigation and can be made to rest upon an objective analysis of human interaction." *Op. cit.,* 19.

4. "In using such examples from life, our purpose is to *illustrate,* not to *describe. . . .* While we have tried to expose the reader to a wealth of illustrative material, the basic framework is analytic rather than descriptive." *Op. cit.,* ix.

5. *Op. cit.,* viii.

6. Harold Stein (ed.): *Cases in Public Administration and Policy Formulation,* New York, Harcourt, Brace and Company, Inc., 1952. Incidentally, this is not the first or only use of the case approach in administrative study. In the late thirties and early forties the Social Science Research Council sponsored a published series of *Case Reports in Public Administration.* These cases, however, were essentially different from the cases under discussion, being short reports of (generally) small problems, including a solution. Individual teachers of public administration, for example, Professor E. O. Stene of the University of Kansas, have prepared cases for their own teaching use. On the case method in public administration, see William Anderson and John M. Gaus, *Research in Public Administration* (Chicago, Public Administration Service, 1945), Chapter 3. See also Stein's introduction, which is an excellent essay on the recent development of administrative study; and his "Human

Relations and Administration—A Review," *Harvard Educational Review,*
    24:59–70 (1954).

7. *Op cit.,* xxvi.

8. See pages xiv–xvii, "Public Administration as Politics," which concludes:
    "The consideration of values in administrative behavior is thus no mere aca-
    demic exercise. Students of public administration must be concerned with
    values. They are observers and they should be capable of dispassionate obser-
    vation; but ultimate neutrality with respect to administrative decisions is self-
    defeating. A lack of concern for the values of public administration is indica-
    tive of a lack of sensitivity; and an insensitive observer can never attain to
    more than a limited insight."

Trends in the Study of Public Administration

Some of the trends in the study of public administration have already been indicated, especially in the preceding discussion of contemporary teaching and training. Let us now, however, address this subject directly, so that the newcomer to the study may view the literature and ideas with which he will be dealing in as broad and clear a perspective as possible.

Present Trends as a Projection of the Past

Present trends can be viewed most clearly when set before the backdrop of the past. The following is a summary—and necessarily oversimplified—statement of the development of the study of public administration, which will then be somewhat expanded: The basic doctrines, the central ideas, of the first textbooks of public administration had appeared and had gained considerable clarity and acceptance by the year 1914. The task and accomplishment of the first textbook-writers was to collect, defend, and systematize these doctrines, and then to build upon them the basic factual categories and data of the day relating to public administration. Having gained the authoritative status of textbook presentation and been given an aura of science, the doctrines, and even the factual categories, tended to be accepted as firm and lasting truths. A synthesis—more, a crystallization—had occurred.

The historical importance of this event was emphasized above, and it cannot in honesty be denied. But while the synthesis was a great achievement, the hardening of doctrines into dogmas, the crystallization, was unfortunate. For a period of more than a decade, from the mid-twenties till the late thirties, students of administration were largely content with the structure that had been erected; so content were they in fact that often they offended colleagues in other fields and disciplines with their manifestations of self-assurance.

In the late thirties and early forties, however, important changes in ideas and shifts in attitudes occurred. The crystallization was broken up, the synthesis dissolved. Why did this take place? We can never be certain why ideas behave as they do, nor of the relation between them and observable events. However, some likely reasons suggest themselves. One is that the thirties was a period of great change and ferment in the field of government. The traumatic experience of the Great Depression brought accepted ideas of all kinds into question. And with the New Deal came important changes in the pattern of government operation, new experiments of various kinds, which were food for thought for all students of political science. The Depression and the New Deal were still with us when the Second World War swept over us, and the momentous events of the past fifteen years have provided a constant stimulus to thinking—and rethinking. It might be added that many academic people participated in the operations of Federal administration in depression, war, and cold war, and had the enlightening experience of mingling study with practice and close observation.[1]

For whatever reasons, in the late thirties and early forties the study of public administration entered into a new period of greatly expanded intellectual activity and growth—to which the files of the *Public Administration Review*, founded in 1940, testify eloquently. We are still in this period of rapid change and growth. At present the boundaries of the interests of students of administration are wider apart, the scope and depth of intellectual interchange with other fields of knowledge is greater, than ever before.

Central Doctrines of Public Administration Prior to 1940

What were the doctrines upon which public administration was based? Four doctrines, closely related, were central. One was that the process of government, analytically considered, consists of two parts only, namely, decision and execution. It is necessary first to decide what should be done— the function and definition of politics—and then to carry out the decision— the role and definition of administration. This may seem a simple and obvious bit of logical analysis, but it must be remembered that the Constitution of the United States (in which, incidentally, the word *administration* does not appear) seems to imply a threefold analysis of the functions of government; and certainly it established a threefold institutional pattern for the Federal government. In any event the important matter for our purpose is the reason why the twofold analysis was accepted and the purposes it served.

The division of the functions of government into two analytically distinct parts served students of the developing study of public administration by enabling them to distinguish and to emphasize that part of government in which they were most interested: execution of decisions, "getting things done." It justified them, for example, in placing a new emphasis upon proper professional or scientific training for administrative work, as against the political spoils system of making administrative appointments; if politics is a function distinct from administration, it should not be permitted to meddle or interfere with administration.

Many of the Founding Fathers of public administration in the progressive era before the First World War, incidentally, were as much interested in a program of political reform as in administrative improvement. Indeed, as noted above, the two interests or objectives were conceived to be closely related and were sought through the same program.[2] On the political side this program sought the creation of two unified, coherent, responsible, and disciplined parties, which could present alternative programs to the voters. On the administrative side the program sought a professional, hierarchical civil service, composed of permanent career members and headed by a single administrator or executive, whether elected or appointed. The voters' proper role was to decide between the alternative parties and programs. The decisions when made then became objectives to be attained by administrative action in the most economical and efficient way. In the period after the First World War students of administration tended to become more specialized, more intent upon administrative improvement in itself, leaving the program of political reform to others. They had declared their independence of politics—a word and realm of low prestige in America, in that day especially.

The second firm doctrine of public administration was that administration can be made into a science, or at the very least lends itself to study in the same manner as do the phenomena of physical science. As students of administration had separated themselves (in their thinking) from politics, a word and realm of low prestige, they associated themselves with science, a word and realm of high prestige. How and why this came about was discussed above and need not be repeated. What is to be noted now is how the strong insistence among writers of the day that administration should become a science fitted nicely with other doctrines of the newly arrived discipline. To declare independence from politics was almost a necessity in making the claim to science plausible, for the rough and tumble of politics seemed completely at odds with the order of the laboratory that connoted science. Or put the other way around, the cool, calculating, rational spirit of science seemed to demand divorce from the passion and chance of the political realm and its seeming disorder.

A third doctrine of public administration in its early synthesis was that scientific study of administration leads to the discovery of principles of administration. These principles were conceived as more or less analogous to the principles or laws of such a physical science as physics or chemistry: The data of administration must be approached in the spirit of thorough, objective inquiry; all facts must be gathered and correlated; and the end product will be firm scientific truths. After all, had not Frederick W. Taylor and others demonstrated that "best ways" *could* be discovered by proper methodology? Why should the approach which had demonstrated its validity in private business not be made to the public's business?[3]

"Principles": Economy and Efficiency

Still another doctrine of early public administration was that economy and efficiency are the central if not the sole goals of administrative study. Getting "good" men into public office is not enough; goodness alone is helpless, even pathetic. What is important is that government be conducted economically and efficiently. And these objectives can be achieved only through scientific study and the discovery and application of the proper principles of administration. Thus the philosophy of early public administration: proper analysis of governmental functions divides administration off from politics; the sphere of administration is one to which science can and should be applied; application of scientific methods of inquiry leads to discovery of principles of organization and management; and these prin-

ciples determine the way in which governmental functions can be administered most economically and efficiently.[4]

In addition to its philosophy, as we have called it, early public administration adopted a number of categories in and by which the factual data of
public administration could be ordered. These categories have already been
indicated in the headings in the tables of contents and by the course titles
given above—such words and concepts as *organization, management, personnel administration, planning, budgeting,* and so forth. An analogy to the
science of biology might be helpful. It too has its doctrines or philosophy—
basic ideas about what it is, how it should proceed, the uses to which it can
be put, its relations to other fields of knowledge. It also has categories by
which the data of biology can be ordered: anatomy, physiology, species,
systems, tropisms, and so forth. In each case the categories are adopted both
because they seem to correspond with natural characteristics of the phenomena and because they are useful in ordering and manipulating the
data.

Changes in Doctrines: 1940 to the Present

We are now in a position to sketch recent and current trends against this
historical background. Since the years of the late thirties, which are something of a transition period or turning point, the philosophy of the study
of public administration has changed significantly. The categories have
changed also. Though the labels have remained largely the same, the data
in all instances have changed enough to make change in meaning per-
ceptible. In some cases the change in meaning is radical; and there are even
some important new labels. The changes in doctrines and categories deserve
our attention.

The rigid, even dogmatic, separation of politics and administration has
been almost wholly abandoned during the past fifteen or twenty years. Indeed, it has become correct to regard administration as a process diffused
or permeated with politics—meaning by the term both the contest for
power (whether or not it is *party* contest) and the making of policy. Partly
this about-face was the result of the empirical investigations of public administration; when closely examined the processes of administration were
revealed to be different from those originally presumed. Partly it was a
result of increasing self-confidence on the part of administrative students;
a wall behind which it could shield itself was no longer felt necessary.
Other factors entered in also, such as a more charitable and optimistic
view of the processes of politics, resulting from considerable improvement
in the moral tone of political life, and the rather widespread popularity of
New Deal politics and policies among students of public administration.

The assertion that public administration is or can be made a science has
come to be made much less often and much less firmly. The reasons for
this are many. One reason is the success of the early firm assertion: to many
it seemed obvious that administration can be studied in a scientific manner
and it seemed unnecessary to assert loudly and at length an obvious truth.
Another reason—as suggested early in this essay—is that controversy over
the scientific nature or possibilities of administrative study came to seem

sterile, scholastic, and hence to be avoided: call administration *both* a science and an art, and get on with it! Still others, perhaps most, were impressed with the case which was made against some of the early notions of scientific method; a critical second look revealed considerable naïveté in the thinking of the Founding Fathers as to what science is and the immediate applicability of its methods in administration. Also, if public administration is permeated by politics, as came to be believed, it seemed less plausible that it is amenable to the techniques of science, at least on any short-term and easy basis.

As is now obvious by implication, the doctrine that there are principles of public administration has been almost wholly abandoned. The word itself is in disrepute, associated as it is with the early and now tarnished if not discredited claim to be science. In the critical period of the thirties and forties it was demonstrated that many of the "principles" were simply not empirically true and that various of them, of seemingly equal validity and acceptance, were contradictory. More importantly, it was demonstrated that many of the principles rested upon or contained what is usually known as the *naturalistic fallacy*, which is the logical fallacy of jumping from the observation of what *is* true to the assertion of what *ought* to be true. The present situation comes to this: students of administration generally feel that their study is important and useful, critically so; that the problems of definition can wait, and problems of methodology cannot be decided a priori but must be tested in use.

The fate of the doctrine of economy and efficiency has been similar to that of principles. Even before the thirties there appeared an occasional argument that economy is too narrow a goal for administrative study; that cheapness is not the proper measure of good government and that efficiency of operation is a better criterion. During the thirties economy was all but discarded, and efficiency in turn was subjected to close scrutiny. Efficiency too then came to be criticized as too narrow, negative, mechanical; writers began to speak of the desirability of "broad social efficiency" and even to argue that other criteria are more important than efficiency, however quali-fied. Nevertheless, economy and efficiency are still with us. Partly this is for a strategic reason; for those (such as legislators) who are called upon to support administrative study, economy and efficiency remain words with power of conviction. Basically, however, economy and efficiency are retained in the present vocabulary of administration because of a suspicion or intui-tion that rejection of them was too hasty, that they signify useful concepts which, properly shaped and restrained, serve desirable purposes.

The Impact of Logical Positivism

Important qualifications must now be made of the generalizations in the above paragraphs. These qualifications must be made because of the work of one of the best known of contemporary students of administration, Herbert A. Simon. In his book, *Administrative Behavior*,[5] published in 1947, Professor Simon introduced to the literature of public administra-tion the doctrines of the school of thought known as logical positivism. Logical positivism is a would-be tough-minded school of thought that asserts its close connection with modern physical science. It abhors meta-physics, dismisses ethics, emphasizes empiricism, places a high premium upon rigorous, logical analysis.

Logical positivism makes a sharp distinction between questions of fact ("is" questions) and questions of value ("ought" questions). Science, by definition, deals only with questions of fact. Propositions of *fact* have as their distinguishing characteristic that they can be empirically verified (or at least in principle verifiable). The realm of *value* is the realm of prefer-ence, of morals or ethics. The distinguishing characteristic of moral and ethical ("ought") propositions is that they cannot be empirically verified.

There is another important distinction made between *theoretical* science and *practical* science. Theoretical science is interested in factual matters in general, so to speak, in establishing what are ordinarily thought of as causal relations between phenomena in an abstract (often mathematical) form, without regard to immediate use. A practical science, however, is concerned with use, and puts the propositions of theoretical science to use. This brings "is" and "ought" categories together in a sense, as it is thought that something *ought* to be done or the practical science would not arise. But this bringing of "is" and "ought" categories together in action does not erase the logical or analytical distinction between the two types of propositions; one type is never transmuted into the other. A proposition in applied science has as a distinguishing characteristic the fact that it is logically resolvable into two propositions, one of value ("such-and-such ought to be done"—often hidden as a premise) and one of fact ("such-and-such can be achieved by this means").

The conceptual apparatus of logical positivism proved in Professor Simon's hands to be a very effective instrument for reasserting and defend-ing the doctrines of public administration which were pictured above as in full retreat. Logical positivism asserts that the data of man's social life lend themselves to scientific study in the same manner as do those of physics or biology, so long as we are careful not to confuse the "is" and the "ought," but confine our attention as scientists strictly to the former.

This position was advanced to meet the charge that the social sciences are essentially different from the physical sciences—and perhaps not sciences at all, since values are an omnipresent aspect of group life. In this view values (as reflected in human behavior) are to be studied empirically, from the outside, just as any other phenomena are studied by a scientist. Thus the scientific nature of administrative study can be reasserted: the phe-nomena of cooperative action can be studied empirically in the same spirit and with the same logical methods as characterize studies of the activities of earthworms or of the mechanism of tropisms. The notion of principles can be reasserted also, since the distinctions between questions of fact and questions of value and between pure science and applied science carefully avoid the naturalistic fallacy. A principle is *either* ethical *or* empirical; a scientific principle is a statement of empirically discovered and demon-strated regularity in phenomenal behavior.

The doctrine of the separation of politics and administration can in turn be reasserted in a different form. Essentially, the early students were correct in emphasizing this distinction, though they did not carry the analysis far enough and were misled into asserting (or at least were believed to be asserting) that politics (values) could be excluded, wholly or largely, from the process of administration. In the logical-positivist system, the administrative process is (or can be) *applied science*, in which knowledge of empirical regularities is being used to achieve whatever goals or values are given. Administration as a process is inevitably value *and* fact, politics *and* administration. Thus, in the logical-positivist view, while the critics were right in asserting the pervasiveness of politics or policy, their criticism went too far and missed the highly important logical—and methodological—distinction between questions of fact and questions of value.

In the same fashion a foundation is provided for the reassertion of economy and efficiency as central concepts or tools of administrative study. In the logical-positivist view the early students again were essentially correct. And the attack against economy and efficiency as narrow and mechanical, and the contrary assertion of the desirability of social efficiency, were merely reflections of a confusion of ends and means in the minds of the critics. Properly conceived, economy and efficiency are measures of comparative effectiveness of means in achieving ends—*any ends*. As such they have an essential role in the applied science of administration.

One can do no more than guess as to the long-range effect of logical positivism on the study of public administration. *Administrative Behavior* has certainly been a widely read and influential work, and all one can say of the present situation is that it has set strong currents flowing counter to those predominant in the forties.

Changes in the Categories of Administrative Study

What changes have there been in the categories of administrative study since the thirties? In general, the labels one finds in the table of contents of today's textbooks resemble those of the textbooks of the thirties. But as stated above, the data under the labels have shifted, perceptibly in all cases, radically in some. And there are a number of changes in the labels themselves. A few of the changes may be indicated, to give some measure of the size and a sense of the direction of recent movements.

One of the two or three most important works on administration to appear in the thirties was titled *Papers on the Science of Administration,* edited by Luther Gulick and Lyndall Urwick. In a noted essay in this volume, Professor Gulick put forward the made-up word POSDCORB as a mnemonic device for recall of the functions of the executive in administration:

> P = Planning
> O = Organizing
> S = Staffing
> D = Directing
> CO = Coordinating
> R = Reporting
> B = Budgeting

Our purpose will be served if we observe what has happened under and to some of these labels and categories.

That *planning* stands first is probably an accident of phonetics, but it occupied a very prominent place indeed in administrative thinking and writing in the mid-thirties. Planning was a very prominent concept in the Scientific Management movement: planning of work flow, production layouts, and so forth. Thus planning would in any case have become a category in the study of public administration by the Scientific Management route, but the Great Depression was responsible for a larger impact on public administration than would otherwise have come about. For in reaction to laissez-faire economic policies, which were thought by many to have brought on or worsened the effects of the depression, planning became highly popular—in fact, in many circles, a fad, even a *mystique*.

From the vantage point of the mid-fifties the enthusiasm for and treatment of planning in the thirties seem very naïve and uncritical. On the one hand, there was a tendency to overlook the fact that both the economic system and the political system of the United States embodied a great deal of planning before the word became popular. Indeed, planning is an important aspect of all complex, modern, social systems; it is an essential ingredient of administration as defined above—rational cooperative endeavor. On the other hand, there was a presumption that we knew more about planning than we actually did: that it was a newly discovered technique or set of rules that would enable us rather quickly and easily to solve the problems of adjusting means to ends in the fantastically complex modern setting.

In the intervening years the treatment of planning by public administration has become mature. We know a great deal more about it: types, techniques, interrelations, problems, and limitations. Other disciplines, particularly economics, have advanced simultaneously in their understanding of planning, and there has been fruitful interchange in the maturation process. At the same time, however, planning has become less prominent as a category. The new is worn off, and there is more free and easy flow of thinking between planning and other categories.

Organizing has undergone changes of similar scope. Professor Gulick's essay in the *papers* presents perhaps the finest summary statement of the organization theory of the thirties. It develops the themes of division of labor and specialization of function, of the need for and means of coordination, the functions of the executive, the differences between line and staff activities, and the advantages and disadvantages of emphasizing (1) purpose, (2) process, (3) people or things, and (4) place in constructing or modifying an organization. This essay also touches upon some of the matters which were to be subjects of much attention at a later date, such as the role of ideas in organization. Nevertheless, the essay presents essentially what might be called organization-chart theory, theory which is characterized by strong emphases upon logical, rational, prescribed relations between persons or functions.

The development of administrative theory during the past fifteen years has been very rapid. The older theories have not been discarded, but have been reset in broader theoretical contexts. (Organization charts still serve important functions, but have slipped from the central position they once held.) Experience and research quickly disclosed phenomena not embraced in the older organization theory; and other disciplines, such as psychology and sociology, were found to have concepts and data of aid in dealing with these phenomena. During the forties, for example, thinking about the staff function was greatly modified by careful observation abetted by insights drawn from social psychology: an element of ideology was found lurking in what had been represented as a scientific conclusion.

Of the various POSDCORB categories *reporting* has changed the most radically. Reporting in the thirties denoted the communication of information up and down the chain of command, and outwardly from the organization to those to whom the organization was responsible. What has happened in this case is the development of communication as an interdisciplinary focus of interests, and almost as a discipline in itself, with the consequent envelopment of reporting in the larger complex of interests. Probably never on an equal footing in administrative usage with its POSDCORB sibs, reporting is an infrequently used category today.

The Current Scene

Seen in broadest perspective the current scene displays much activity, change, and progress: certainly today the study of public administration is not stagnant, whatever may be said against it. On the one hand there is a drive forward on the factual side. The search continues for ever more accurate conceptual apparatuses, more useful models, statements of empirical uniformities which are precise, rigorous. On the other hand, there is a newly awakened interest in the value side of public administration. This interest in the value or "ought" aspects of public administration is related to the rather far-reaching abandonment of the politics-administration dichotomy commented on above, and to a belief that values inevitably permeate administration as a process and that the study of public administration must take account of this fact.

The interest in the value component of public administration has taken several forms. One prominent form is the amendment of curricula by the introduction or extension of courses in public policy. Another form is the current enthusiasm for the study of cases—careful, photographic accounts of administrative episodes. While the use of cases in administrative study is defended on several grounds, the title of the widely used *Public Administration and Policy Development*, edited by Harold Stein, indicates the undoubted desire somehow to embrace the value component within our study.[6]

The following two chapters of this essay are in part commentaries on the theme of the preceding two paragraphs. The next section deals with the relationships between the study of public administration and other disciplines; for the most notable consequence of the recent pursuit of the factual or scientific has been the development of fruitful interrelations with other disciplines. The chapter following is in turn given over to a survey of some of the problems posed by the conscious introduction of ethical problems into the discipline of public administration.

Footnotes to Chapter Four. Trends in the Study of Public Administration

1. No better example of this could be cited than the textbook *Elements of Public Administration* (New York, Prentice-Hall, Inc., 1946) edited by Fritz Morstein Marx. All fifteen of the contributing authors participated in administration during the Second World War, and all but two had been or are now in Academia.

2. One of the classics of American political science is *Politics and Administration* (New York, The Macmillan Co., 1900) by Frank Goodnow. This work developed the general philosophy sketched here and for decades was often assumed by students of administration to have proved that administration could be and should be separated from both partisan politics and the making of policy.

3. See W. F. Willoughby, "The Science of Public Administration," in *Essays in Political Science* (Baltimore, The Johns Hopkins University Press, 1937) edited by J. M. Mathews and James Hart, for an example of the thinking I am trying to outline, with respect both to science and to principles.

4. See Luther Gulick's essay, "Science, Values and Public Administration," the concluding essay in *Papers on the Science of Administration* (New York, Institute of Public Administration, 1937) edited by Gulick and L. Urwick, for the classic, orthodox statement of the principle of efficiency.

5. Herbert A. Simon: *Administrative Behavior* (New York, The Macmillan Co., 1947). Professor Simon's book is subtitled: *A Study of Decision-Making Processes in Administrative Organization.* See also *Public Administration* (New York, Alfred A. Knopf, Inc., 1950) by Herbert A. Simon, Donald W. Smithburg, and Victor A. Thompson, Foreword and Chapter 1, for a spelling out of the implications of logical positivism (though it is not here mentioned by name) for administrative study.

6. The development of the doctrines and categories of the study of public administration down to about 1940 can be traced in more detail in the author's *The Administrative State: A Study of the Political Theory of American Public Administration* (New York, The Ronald Press Company, 1948); and changes since that date are outlined and documented in the author's "Administrative Theory in the United States: A Survey and Prospect," *Political Studies* 2:70–86 (1954).

chapter five

Administrative Study and the Social Sciences

In an earlier day public administration was eager to assert its independence. This was natural and understandable; normal adolescence is characterized by assertions of independence. With the achievement of separate textbooks, courses, curricula, and professional societies, however, came a feeling of security and maturity, a willingness to recognize old debts and bonds, and a healthy eagerness to reach out toward new fields of knowledge.

During the past decade increasing attention has been given to the possible contributions of other disciplines to the special interests of administrative study, notably of the other social sciences. At the present time there is considerable—and important—interaction. Writers professionally associated with such disciplines as sociology and social psychology publish in the journals of public administration. Often they are addressing their attention directly to phenomena in, or related to, administration that have been the focus of study by students of administration; but they have a different perspective and bring to bear different conceptual tools.

Increasingly too students of administration are turning their attention to these outside fields; the evidence appears in new research orientations, different language, and of course in footnote and bibliography. Sometimes it is research findings that are accepted; for example, findings concerning worker morale and productivity. Sometimes it is research methods, or techniques; for example, the use of symbolic logic in stating organizational theory. Sometimes it is concepts or models; for example, the idea of bureaucracy as an "ideal typical" form of organization. Often it is only a subtle, but unmistakable and important, change of emphasis. What follows is a brief indication of some of the present interactions between administrative study and other disciplines.

Political Science[1]

Public administration may be, and in some sense certainly is, a part of political science. But within political science are various clusters of interest that relate to public administration in various ways. One of the clusters of interest may be designated Parties, Politics, and Public Opinion. In the past decade or so, paralleling the dropping away of the old division between politics and administration, there has been increasing liaison with this area. John M. Gaus states the current attitude of what is certainly a large majority of public-administration students when he states,

"A theory of public administration means in our time a theory of politics too."[2] Exchange with this area, particularly with the public-opinion area, is fostered by the fact that it too has been affected by some of the currents— label them roughly *behavioral research*—that have affected public administration. Opinion-polling techniques and such devices as content analysis are of importance in both fields.

With the areas of studies in international relations and comparative government there is important interaction—in sharp contrast to the situation fifteen years ago. The change is undoubtedly attributable chiefly to the interests and activities stimulated by the Second World War, the Cold War, and the enhanced role of the United States in world affairs. Legalistic and formal treatments of international organizations have been supplemented by the concepts of administrative study; and public administration has been given not only a new level, the international, but a new dimension, the intercultural. An examination of books in comparative government discloses an increased interest in public administration, and within the field of public administration, comparative administration is a burgeoning field.

With the other areas of political science relations are not at present very close. There is little creative interaction. With the field of study of public law there are still strained relations stemming from the early attempt of public administration to assert a management point of view as against the traditional approach of legal rights, duties, and procedures; and from what students of administration are prone to regard as an offensive combination of aridity and arrogance in the lawyer's approach to administration. Since contemporary law is in many ways a progressive field[3] and since public administration is inevitably surrounded and conditioned by legal norms, the continuing estrangement is unfortunate.

In the early days of public administration its relations with the study of state and local government were very close. However, because of the focus of interest on national government during the past generation, and perhaps for other reasons, such as a tendency of the state and local area to become self-contained, there is little creative interaction at present here.

With the area of political theory, relations of public administration have never been close or cordial. Owing to its practical or empirical origins, public administration was at first hostile to theory and philosophy; and the students of general political theory were in turn repelled by this attitude and inclined to regard administration as beneath their note—a field for mechanics. Lately, students of administration have been reaching out toward political theory; and have been themselves contributing in an important way to political theory. It is to be hoped that the students of general political theory will turn to administration. In the era of the Administrative State they cannot do otherwise if they are to avoid increasing sterility in some of their endeavors.

History

In its early period administrative study was highly unhistorical. The study of history was associated with a bookish approach to life, whereas the early students of administration were moved by the maxim of the naturalist, Jean Henri Fabre: "Study nature, not books." Taylor's meticulous examinations of current phenomena were the model, the time-and-motion study the symbol. For a generation or more the emphasis was upon getting out of the library and into the laboratory of life.

This emphasis was not misplaced, given the situation in which it occurred. Certainly the study of administration could not have advanced to its present level without breaking the chains of the past. During the past ten or fifteen years, however, there has arisen a new interest in history.

Why has this taken place? One reason has to do with inherent difficulties of applying the established methods of the physical sciences, such as the controlled experiment, in the social field. Lacking exact testing of hypotheses under controlled conditions the social scientist rather naturally turns to the record of the past for comparisons. He knows, if he is wise, that history never repeats and that such comparisons are never exact, but he still believes that the careful use of history adds to his understanding of present data.

Another reason has to do with changing fashions in the writing of history. History can of course be written from a multitude of points of view. The dominant emphasis in the writing of history when administrative study was born was on political, military, and legal data: the story of kings and presidents, battles and wars, constitutions and laws, did not seem very relevant to administration. During the past fifty or seventy-five years the study of history has been enriched by many new hypotheses and perspectives. Economic history, social history, scientific and technological history, and intellectual history have been widely explored and greatly expanded. Moreover, a number of professional historians have turned their attention to the history of administration itself—in church, state, business, the military, and wherever else it has developed.

Whatever the reasons, students of administration are undoubtedly much more interested in history—so far as they deem it to relate to administration at least—than they were a generation ago. One very notable symbol of the change in attitude may be cited: The record of our war administration in the First World War is extremely meager, whereas that of our war administration in the Second World War is very rich. A main reason for this difference is that students of administration used their influence to get the administrative history of the Second World War written. While the war was in progress official historians were at work "capturing and recording" administrative experience for future use in administrative study.

What can we learn from administrative history? Here we will do well to quote from a perceptive essay, "The Uses of History,"[4] by Harvey C. Mansfield: "What kinds of generalizations can be derived from administrative history? Tentatively, I suggest that for our purposes at least three types, or levels of particularity, may usefully be distinguished. For convenience I shall call them philosophical observations, analytical or problem-solving techniques, and administrative techniques." By "philosophical observations" is meant general observations or conclusions which, though they do not decide concrete cases, "help establish a mood of understanding in those who have the job to do again." By "analytical or problem-solving techniques" is meant "middle-gauged" lessons or conclusions concerning administration proper or the economic, political, or legal milieu. And by "administrative techniques" is meant "narrow-gauged" lessons: "They are of the if-you-have-to-do-it-again-do-it-this-way variety of lessons, on a par with the techniques of the factory, the department store, or the farmer cultivating his crops."

Cultural Anthropology

Cultural anthropology as a field of study has been primarily concerned with primitive or simpler societies in which administration as rational social cooperation is not very far advanced. It may seem peculiar, therefore, that it is mentioned at all in this discussion of the contribution of other areas to administrative study.

Actually, the uses of anthropology to the student of administration are complementary to those of history. For as history provides, for the study of rational cooperative endeavor, the perspective of civilized societies chronologically, anthropology provides the perspective of primitive societies geographically. Much knowledge and insight on the range, combinations, and permutations of human cooperation are gained by surveying the wide cultural spectrum embraced by anthropology.

The central concept of culture is actually broader than its traditional association with simpler societies suggests. As a general concept it is applicable (as we hope was demonstrated in Chapter One) to complex civilized societies as well; and while much care is needed when extending analysis and conclusions from simple to complex societies lest error and folly creep in, the discipline of anthropology is broadening its interests and refining its techniques to accomplish this objective. In fact many studies of administrative problems in complex societies are now being made by anthropologists, as a perusal of journals in this field quickly reveals.[5] The broadening of the range of interest of administrative study by the technical assistance programs that have followed the Second World War is relevant here; anthropology has a special contribution to make to these important cross- or intercultural cooperative endeavors.

Sociology

While sociology is a discipline in its own right, it is in a sense a combination of history and anthropology. It embraces in its interests all societies, simple and complex, historical and contemporary; it uses the data of both history and anthropology for its own conceptual systems; and it might be said that it processes the data of history and anthropology for readier application in administrative study.

Sociology concerns itself with the most general problems of cause and effect in human societies, and the student of administration is often able to get from the literature of sociology a useful hypothesis or revealing insight—for example, concerning the relationship between the rationality of the medium of exchange in a society and its general capacity for rational social action. More narrowly, sociology concerns itself with such categories as status, class, power, occupation, family, caste, prestige, and so forth; and the relevance of such categories for a well-developed administrative study is becoming increasingly clear. We are becoming more and more aware that human cooperative systems are shaped and controlled by their environment, their ecology. Sociologists—some of whom are deeply interested in administration—have had much to do with this developing emphasis.

A brief examination of the concept of bureaucracy will illustrate the usefulness of the sociological perspective, and how sociologists process the data of history and anthropology. The best-known conceptualization of bureaucracy in sociology is that of Max Weber, a German scholar of a generation ago. Weber's scholarship ranged across cultures and up and down the centuries. One of his significant conclusions was that under certain conditions of human culture bureaucracy tends to emerge. Bureaucracy in this sense is an institution, or complex of institutions, having certain definable, describable characteristics. Specifically and very briefly, in its fully developed or ideal state, it is characterized by:

1. Fixed and official jurisdictions which are ordered by rules (laws or regulations).
2. The principle of hierarchy (super- and subordination).
3. The keeping of extensive, careful, and usually secret records.
4. Professional, or at least thorough, training for participation.
5. Separation of office or work place from domicile; and full-time attention to one institution or position.
6. Operation according to rules more or less stable and exhaustive.

Now this is obviously a sketch of what we are familiar with as administration in business, government, or elsewhere; and there may be wonder that it is thought to be a useful contribution. But the point is that Weber cast much light upon the historical and cultural conditions under which what we may think of as normal administrative arrangements emerge, and hence on how by testing and exploration we can learn to achieve—or perhaps change—such arrangements if we wish. It is impossible to read Weber's writings on bureaucracy without a feeling that one now stands outside his culture and can observe in this perspective previously hidden but significant relationships between administration and, for example, educational systems, economic systems, and family systems.

As another example of the usefulness of a sociological perspective we may take the concept of *cooptation*. This concept was developed and applied in a study of the TVA by Philip Selznick,[6] in what has proved to be one of the most interesting and valuable studies of recent years.

The general problem posed by the study was the relationship of a formal organization to its setting and the adaptive responses made by an organization in order to survive and grow: "the security of the organization as a whole in relation to social forces in its environment." Cooptation was conceived as *one type* of adaptive response and was defined as "the process of absorbing new elements into the leadership or policy-determining structure of an organization as a means of averting threats to its stability or existence."[7] A further distinction was made between formal and informal types of cooptation.

In this study the findings were that the TVA had by cooptation allied itself with and taken in certain socioeconomic elements in its environment, namely, the more prosperous farmers, the Farm Bureau Federation, the county agents, and the extension service of the land-grant schools. The results were many, important, and pervasive. In terms of politics this brought the TVA into alliance with certain elements, for example, the parts of the Department of Agriculture favorable to the land-grant schools and the extension service; and into opposition with certain parts of the departments of Agriculture and the Interior interested in rural low-income groups and in conservation. In terms of policy, there were resulting emphases already suggested.

This study is sometimes interpreted as muckraking, an attack upon the integrity and good name of an agency that has been highly regarded by liberals. Such an interpretation misses the point and purpose. In Selznick's view, the TVA *had no option* whether it would engage in cooptation; cooptation was necessary for survival and to accomplish *any* objectives. The goals that TVA leaders chose to put first were public-power goals. These goals TVA largely achieved, but the price of success was the relinquishment of many other goals that perhaps were good and *might* have been achieved. The point is—if the study was correct in its facts and conclusions and is sustained by other studies of the same phenomena—that *this is the way formal organizations work*, and the study of administration is enriched by the knowledge.[8]

Social Psychology

Administration has been defined as cooperation and thus by definition as a social activity. The study of psychology as it relates to the social is therefore relevant to administrative study. Students of administration are interested in many of the data and findings of social psychology, and social psychologists find administrative phenomena an important area of study.

There is an easy flow of data and concepts, and considerable intermingling of personnel among social anthropology, sociology, and social psychology. This is very noticeable in study projects in business or factory administration: there are many study projects or experiments to which the terms *plant psychology, industrial anthropology,* and *industrial sociology* are about equally applicable. Whatever the label, such studies are of interest and value to the student of public administration. For example, one of the more recent trends in the study of public administration is to give more attention to what is usually called in the public administration literature *informal organization*. The student of administration will find that there is a rich literature on *primary groups* or *face-to-face groups* dealing with phenomena he has come recently to recognize under his own label.

One of the more interesting books on the subject of the face-to-face group may be noted: *The Human Group* (New York, Harcourt, Brace & Company, 1950), by George C. Homans. This is a review of several field studies of face-to-face groups in very different social and cultural settings, for example, a boys' street-corner gang and a kinship group in Polynesia. Homans is seeking for the constants in face-to-face group behavior, and presents for reflection and testing a series of hypotheses, such as the following:

An increasing specialization of activities will bring about a decrease in the range of interaction of a person concerned with any one of these activities and will limit the field in which he can originate interaction.

As the range of a man's interaction declines, as he interacts less often with the leaders of his group, and as the field in which he exercises authority becomes more limited, his social rank will decline.[9]

These hypotheses are presented here without the wealth of supporting comment that Homans gives them; an intervening hypothesis has been omitted. But what is presented here will surely put the mind of one interested and experienced in administration at work: Is this true or false? What in my experience or study would seem to substantiate it? what to refute it?

Other examples of the use of social psychology are easily found. Studies of leadership, for example, throw light on this phenomenon in administration. Studies of role-playing illumine such problems in administration as indoctrination of new employees; tests and measurements aid in recruiting and promoting; and polling and sampling techniques make possible more rational calculations by making clearer the consequences of alternative courses of action.

Economics

The study of economics and the study of administration touch and even join together at a number of places. Public finance, budgeting, and fiscal administration are subjects of proper interest to both disciplines, and in each of them the disciplines can each learn from the other. Taxes, for example, vary not only in their economic aspects, but in their administrative feasibility; a budget is both a major instrument of administrative control and a major factor in the economy it covers.

The interchange—present and potential—between economics and public administration runs, however, far beyond the areas, such as public finance, that they share in a formal sense. There is a tendency for some parts of political science and economics to converge. This tendency results in large part from the current in politicoeconomic life toward the increased role of government in economic life during the past generation or two. The mixed economy of our day, though still comparatively free, is very far from that of the nineteenth century—and still further from nineteenth-century classical economic theory. The convergence in study or concepts is most striking perhaps in Robert A. Dahl and Charles E. Lindblom's *Politics, Economics and Welfare*. In this work the authors argue for a return to political economy as a working area or discipline, and use the current concepts of their respective fields of political science and economics to demonstrate how this might be done.[10]

One of the developments in economic study that brings it closer to political science in general and public administration in particular is the study of economic *institutions*, such as the modern corporation, and the development of what is referred to as *theory of the firm* (as distinguished, for example, from theory concerning the individual as an economic atom, and theory of the economy as a whole—*macroeconomic* theory). When corporations, firms, or companies are studied as systems of power[11] or equilibrating systems or miniature economies,[12] then obviously such study begins to parallel—and to converge with—those of business administration and of public administration.[13]

Business Administration

Business administration and public administration grew up as allied disciplines, and their mutual borrowings, especially those of public administration from business administration, have been large. The inspiring drive of many of the Founding Fathers of public administration was the drive to apply business methods to government. If one thinks of the Scientific Management movement as business administration, then the debt of public administration to business administration is large indeed.

In the 1920's and 1930's developments occurred at the Harvard Business School which should be noted even in this brief survey. These developments center in the work and writings of Elton Mayo[14] and some experiments carried on at the Hawthorne plant of the Western Electric Company. These experiments were conducted to test factors governing worker productivity. The results showed—contrary to expectations—that the *social* condition of the workers was more important than the *physical* conditions (within reasonable limits). The working *group* was discovered to have an importance hitherto unsuspected.

The implications of the studies spread in ever-widening circles, transforming the study of industrial management and reaching into other fields. (In a sense the development could be described as a refutation of Scientific Management; but in another sense it was but an enlargement of it, applying objective study to still more phenomena.) Several of the social sciences were stimulated and enriched, public administration included. The study of face-to-face groups, discussed above, owes much to the Hawthorne experiments.

While interaction between public administration and business administration continues, the relationship between the two is so well established that it lacks some of the excitement of more recent discoveries. Two examples of recent interaction or borrowing may be noted, however. One of these is the case approach to administrative study and teaching. Both disciplines have been experimenting in this area, with cross-boundary stimulation and criticism. The other example concerns democracy. Democracy has been primarily a political concept historically, and it would appear logical that it might be borrowed by business administration from public administration. As it has happened—for various reasons which cannot be here explored —the reverse is nearer to the actual situation. Several writers identified primarily with business administration have been concerned with the development of democratic techniques and the realization of democratic values *within administration,* and their writings have been influential in some degree in the study of public administration.

Other Disciplines

This discussion of relationships with other disciplines is merely suggestive, not exhaustive. It can be closed by noting that the disciplines singled out for attention, while perhaps those currently most important, are by no means all of those with which there is some kind or degree of interchange. Communications and the behavior sciences are, for example, two contemporary foci of interest with which there is intellectual commerce. Various physical sciences and technologies supply grist for the mill of the administrative student. Indeed, no discipline is without its relevance for administration—and administrative study has relevance for every discipline.

Footnotes to Chapter Five. Administrative Study and the Social Sciences

1. This review of political science follows closely the author's discussion of this subject in "Administrative Theory in the United States: A Survey and Prospect," *Political Studies* 2:70–86 (1954).

2. "Trends in the Theory of Public Administration," *Public Administration Review* 10:161–168 (1950).

3. See the presentation of this point of view in Nathan Grundstein's "Law and the Morality of Administration," *George Washington Law Review* 21:265–310 (1953).

4. *Public Administration Review* 11:51–56 (1951). Some of the official and unofficial (privately published—"semiofficial" seems to fit some) war histories may be cited: Walter W. Wilcox: *The Farmer in the Second World War*, Ames, Iowa State College Press, 1947; Ray S. Cline: *Washington Command Post: The Operations Division*, Washington, D.C., Government Printing Office, 1951; James P. Baxter, *Scientists Against Time*, Boston, Little, Brown & Co., 1946; Bureau of the Budget: *The United States at War: Development and Administration of the War Program by the Federal Government*, Washington, D.C., Government Printing Office, 1946; and H. M. Somers: *Presidential Agency, OWMR*, Cambridge, Harvard University Press, 1950.

5. *Human Organization*, formerly *Applied Anthropology*, may be cited in this connection, though it is not a journal of anthropology in any strict sense. In fact it illustrates the confluence of the streams of activity in several disciplines concerned primarily with empirical or behavioral studies; it is subtitled: *Studies towards the Integration of the Social Sciences*. The following titles, selected at random, indicate studies of interest to students of public administration: "A Study of a Rumor: Its Origin and Spread," 1:464–486 (1948) by Leon Festinger *et al.*; "The Dynamics of Power," 5:37–64 (1952) by Ronald Lippitt *et al.*; "The Contributions of a Discussion Leader to the Quality of Group Thinking: The Effective Use of Minority Opinions," 5:277–288 (1952) by N. R. F. Maier and Allen R. Solem; and "The Effect of Changing the Leadership of Small Work Groups," 6:25–44 (1953).

One of the anthropological works most interesting to the student of administration is A. H. Leighton's *The Governing of Men: General Principles and Recommendations Based on Experience at a Japanese Relocation Camp* (Princeton, Princeton University Press, 1945). The narrative is interesting in itself as a case study, and there is a long series of stimulating hypotheses.

6. Philip Selznick: *TVA and the Grass Roots: A Study in the Sociology of Formal Organization*, Berkeley and Los Angeles, University of California Press, 1949.

7. *Op. cit.*, 259.

8. In connection with sociology, it will be useful to look at the volume *Reader in Bureaucracy* (Glencoe, Ill., The Free Press, 1952) edited by R. K. Merton, A. P. Gray, B. Hockey, and H. C. Selvin. The book runs beyond sociology, demonstrating the lack of firm lines in the study of administrative phenomena. The chapter headings are worth quoting:

   Bureaucracy: Theoretical Conceptions
   Bases for the Growth of Bureaucracy
   Bureaucracy and Power Relations
   The Structure of Bureaucracy
   Status Systems and Gradations of Prestige
   Conflicts of Authority
   Recruitment and Advancement
   The Bureaucrat
   Social Pathologies of Bureaucracy
   Field Methods for the Study of Bureaucracy

9. Homans, *The Human Group*, 406–407. Homans has what he ventures to call rules of leadership in his study:

   1. The leader will maintain his own position.
   2. The leader will live up to the norms of his group.
   3. The leader will lead.
   4. The leader will not give orders that will not be obeyed.
   5. In giving orders, the leader will use established channels.
   6. The leader will not thrust himself upon his followers on social occasions.
   7. The leader will neither blame nor, in general, praise a member of his group before other members.
   8. The leader will take into consideration the total situation.
   9. In maintaining discipline, the leader will be less concerned with inflicting punishment than with creating the conditions in which the group will discipline itself.
   10. The leader will listen.
   11. The leader will know himself.

Incidentally there has been a recent shift in emphasis and conclusions in the study of leadership by the psychologists. Earlier studies proceeded largely on the basis of trait analysis of leaders, trying to find the constants in terms of personal characteristics. Later studies, somewhat influenced by what is called the field concept, have put the emphasis upon the situation in which the leader leads. Without wholly discounting earlier studies, the present tendency is to conclude that leadership is situational or specific, that is to say, the leader is not successful by virtue of traits or characteristics he can carry to other situations, but by virtue of a special relationship to particular situations.

10. See William J. Baumol: *Welfare Economics and the Theory of the State,* Cambridge, Harvard University Press, 1952; and Gunnar Myrdal: *The Political Element in the Development of Economic Theory,* London, Routledge & Kegan Paul, Ltd., 1953.

11. See Robert A. Brady: *Business as a System of Power,* New York, Columbia University Press, 1943; and Robert A. Gordon: *The Business Leadership in the Large Corporations,* Washington, Brookings Institution, 1945.

12. The idea of an organization or administrative system as an equilibrating input-output system is one with various sources and manifestations, but certainly some of the impulse and language comes from economics. See *The Organizational Revolution: A Study in the Ethics of Economic Organization* by Kenneth E. Boulding. Cf. Chester I. Barnard: *The Functions of the Executive* (Cambridge, Harvard University Press, 1947).

13. Another type of interchange with economics is illustrated by Herbert A. Simon's application of economic concepts to the decision-making process in administration, in *Administrative Behavior; A Study of Decision-Making Processes in Administrative Organization.*

14. See his series of little books: *The Human Problems of an Industrial Civilization,* first published 1933; reprinted, Cambridge, Harvard University Press, 1946; *The Social Problems of an Industrial Civilization* (1945); *The Political Problem of an Industrial Civilization* (1947).

There is a voluminous literature on the Hawthorne experiments. See especially, F. J. Roethlisberger: *Management and Morale,* Cambridge, Harvard University Press, 1950; and F. J. Roethlisberger and W. J. Dickson: *Management and the Worker,* Cambridge, Harvard University Press, 1950.

The files of *Fortune* magazine should be perused by anyone studying the development of business-administration thought.

chapter six

The Value Problem in Administrative Study

There has been comment at various points in previous chapters bearing on the value problem in administrative study. What is the value problem? It is the problem of choice between goals, and of choice between means of realizing goals. It is the problem of the *should* or the *ought*.

The study of administration is concerned with the discovery of the relative costs of goals and means. (Incidentally, it is most realistic and fruitful to think of means as intermediate goals, and goals—except the ultimate goals we state in abstract terms—as means to further goals.) But the cost factor alone seldom if ever yields the answer. Given either different or identical computations of costs or of efficiencies for plausible alternatives, a wise decision will weigh factors other than cost or efficiency. And after all facts are gathered, there remains an ultimate element of choice in every decision that is beyond rationality in the sense in which this term is used in this essay.

In concrete form the value problem is posed, for example, when an administrator is deciding what influence or weight (if any) is to be given to the claims of competing interest groups in determining a program in such a matter as housing, health, or crop controls. Or when an administrator is deciding upon an assignment of office space or scarce telephone facilities. Or when a budget officer is deciding which recommendations for increased expenditures (if any) he will support. Or when a personnel official is deciding which type of educational preparation he will favor in a recruitment program. And even when an administrator is deciding whether to grant his secretary's request for next Monday off.

Genesis of the Contemporary Value Problem: The Politics-Administration Dichotomy

The value problem in administrative study should be seen in relation to the early doctrine that politics and administration are separable phenomena, and to the later and contemporary trend to abandon this doctrine. For those who accepted the doctrine that politics and administration are separable phenomena there was no value problem: it was defined out of existence. According to the early interpretation, value was assigned to politics. It was conceived to be the function of politics to weigh evidence and sift issues and finally decide upon a course of action directed toward a goal. It was the function of administration then to realize this goal in the most economical and efficient way. In general, at least, this difference in function corresponded in the minds of its adherents to a difference in governmental organs and agents. Politics was identified primarily with the legislative body, administration primarily with the departments and the chief executive.

In this scheme of things values—the "ought" aspect of decision-making—could be taken for granted. The norms or goals of action were thought of as specified *for* administration, not *by* it. Administration functioned purely as an instrument. Writing in the 1880's Woodrow Wilson put it thus: we can learn from a murderous rogue his technique of sharpening a knife without borrowing also his intent to commit murder. So can we learn, he argued, efficient techniques of administration from the autocracies of Europe and use these efficient techniques the better to realize the goals of our democracy.

This point of view held sway until the 1930's, but has since largely been abandoned. Increasingly careful study and thought revealed that administrative organs and agents were in fact making policy. It is now accepted by virtually all students that administrative organs and agents help to determine the norms or goals set by law for administrative action. They do this in various ways, including submission of legislative proposals. It is also recognized that the norms or goals set by law are usually so abstract and indeterminate that the administering organs or agents have a wide range of action open to them. They can in fact make policy by deciding in the concrete case what is to be done—or not done. Moreover, it is generally recognized that policy is made not just in the front office, but at least in small degree by administrators down into the lowest echelons.

As noted in the discussion of current trends in administrative study, recognition of these facts has resulted in a tendency toward admission of policy into the administrative curriculum. If administrators must make policy decisions then they should be put on notice and prepared to do so consciously and intelligently. Recent years have witnessed an increase of courses in public policy, a new or greatly enlarged concern with decision-making processes, and even some overt concern with administrative morality and ethics.

If the practice of administration—and some would say, its study too—involves the making of decisions into which values enter, then what values? What substantive values or preferences should be stressed? What procedures for discovering, delineating, and weighing values should be used? How should the values—or at least the techniques for dealing with values—be inculcated? It is this cluster of questions that constitutes the value problem in public administration.

The Problem in Broad Perspective

It will be useful to view this problem in public administration in a broad perspective. It is not a problem of public administration alone. It is one shared with political science, and beyond that with the other social sciences. Indeed, it reaches beyond the social sciences and into many roots and branches of modern life.

The social sciences of today developed from currents set flowing by the eighteenth-century Enlightenment. The dominant philosophies of the Enlightenment were natural-rights and utilitarianism. While there were important differences between the school of natural rights and utilitarianism, both philosophies shared some basic ideas and sentiments. They were alike in presuming that answers to "ought" questions could be found by examining certain facts, however much they disagreed on what should be examined and the method of examination. They were also alike in the dominant notions associated with both as to what directions public policy should take. These notions were, or evolved into, the complex of ideas associated today with the expression liberal democratic.

In Western countries perhaps the most important philosophic movement of the twentieth century has been toward the separation of the categories of fact and value, the "is" and the "ought." This movement is prominently associated with the school or outlook designated logical positivism or logical empiricism. The general tenor and some of the basic postulates of this movement were noted above in the discussion of current trends. As a movement it claims close identification with science.

The movement toward a separation of the categories of fact and value is broader than logical positivism, however, and it has also come from the opposite philosophic pole, the idealist. Some idealist philosophers, in reaction to the materialist ethos of modern science, have emphasized that attention to the "is" of facts can not alone determine for us either the good or the right.

The split between fact and value, "is" and "ought," creates problems for the social scientist. It makes for a split personality. On the one hand the social scientist, as a general rule, carries along the baggage of moral beliefs he has received from the past, the beliefs constituting the liberal democratic outlook. On the other hand the original philosophical foundations for these beliefs have disappeared, and no philosophy has gained general acceptance as a suitable alternative. So the social scientist lives in two worlds lacking an organic connection. There is the world of the facts, with which he is concerned as a scientist. And there is the world of his ideology or values. Since his value system cannot be justified in terms of facts, and his professional dedication is thought of as one to Fact, he is without justification for carrying his value system into his science. But as we have seen, administration as a process is now pictured as the making of myriad decisions into every one of which values must enter.

The Logical-Positivist View

It must quickly be said that what is here posed as a problem is only a pseudo problem to the logical positivist. Indeed, in his eyes the virtue and significance of his way of viewing things is that it provides a sophisticated and subtle set of concepts which enables him to treat values as values, facts as facts, and to deal with both together when they appear together—as they do in the decision-making process.

If (in the logical-positivist view) values are unverifiable, this is unfortunate. Their unverifiability removes them from the realm of science, for science deals only with questions of What is the case? But that values cannot be verified does not prevent the development of social science; social science deals with questions of What is the case? That is to say, it deals with verifiable empirical regularities in the social realm, just as physical science deals with verifiable empirical regularities in the physical realm. (In fact, the social realm is also physical.) To be sure, when the science is applied instead of pure, when it is being put to use in the achievement of goals, the value element enters: every decision is a bringing together of factual and valuational elements. (Propositions in pure science take the logical form "A is followed by B." Propositions in applied science take the logical form "If it is desired to achieve X, then Y should be done.")

The administrator's role is conceived as analogous to that of the engineer. As the engineer applies his science or technology to the realization of ends which he accepts as given or his own for the time, so does the administrator. In a democracy, on this view, the goals of the administrator are given by the accepted process of democratic politics. Of course, ethical problems may arise and confront the administrator; so do they arise and confront the engineer. But the ethical problems that may arise must not be confused with the technical problems of realizing given goals with an economy of means.

The case presented by logical positivism is plausible and persuasive. Nevertheless, a considerable number of students of social science find it of limited truth or usefulness. Some of the arguments that have been presented against it are as follows:

(1) Logical positivism mistakes a distinction in logic for a distinction in life. While it is possible in the study or laboratory to divide all reality into two neat pieces, reality as it is experienced in the process of living is a seamless web. In the decision-making process, fact and value are joined not merely mechanically, but organically. Water is analytically hydrogen and oxygen. This is useful information. But *as water* it has important qualities quite different from its constituent elements.

(2) What is presented as an instrument of analysis becomes inevitably a program of action—with unfortunate results. Adequate presentation of the argument here goes far beyond the available space. Summary presentation of a few propositions must suffice.

(*a*) "A radical separation of fact and value—too often identified with the logical distinction between fact *statements* and preference *statements*—encourages the divorce of means and ends"[1]—which is what administration is about. For the one-time institutional separation of policy and administration, logical positivism substitutes a logical separation of value and fact that is equally misleading. The result is an "excessive or premature technological orientation. This posture is marked by a concentration on ways and means. The ends of action are taken for granted, viewed as essentially unproblematic 'givens' in organization-building and decision-making. The enterprise is conceived of as a tool whose goals are set externally. This need not be a problem, if tasks are narrowly and sharply defined, as in the case of a typist pool or machine-records unit. At this extreme, the organization is totally absorbed into a technological context, and leadership is dispensable. However, as we move to areas where self-determination becomes increasingly important—where 'initiative' must be exercised—the specification of goals loses its innocence. In particular, if a leadership acts as if it had no creative role in the formulation of ends, when in fact the situation demands such a role, it will fail, leaving a history of uncontrolled, opportunistic adaptation behind it."[2]

(b) While they are very knowledgeable about the value premises of others, logical positivists may be naïve about their own. This situation may occur because, in their eagerness to separate facts from value, they presume they have removed their own research from any value contamination. Actually, however, careful empirical examination will disclose that values have entered by the back door. What is being researched is valued, or it would not be researched.

(c) Logical-positivist research lends itself to the bias or uses of elitism. Logical positivism is value blind. That is to say, while logical positivists inevitably have value systems, these value systems are accidental; and whatever research into facts may be undertaken, this research also has only a fortuitous relationship with any set of values. Therefore, the logical positivist in effect wears a "For Hire" sign. Those most able to hire him are those with most money and power, and their purpose is likely to be the natural one of perpetuating their superior positions.

(3) The value neutrality of means asserted by logical positivism is false. This argument perhaps cannot be made against all logical positivists. Some acknowledge the necessity of positing ends and conceive of their research as scientific inquiry into the way these ends can be realized. Some, however, assert that it is meaningful to inquire into the efficiency of means in the abstract; that knowledge of the efficient reaching of ends can be used to reach any ends efficiently. Against this point of view it is argued, first, that the efficiency of any mean is relative to particular ends. It is argued, secondly, that logical positivism fosters an instrumentalist view of means which is false to life. That is to say, means come to be valued in themselves for the satisfactions they produce immediately; and when examined closely and realistically the distinction between ends and means becomes unreal.

(4) Despite its firm commitment to the ideal of Science, the effect of logical positivism paradoxically may be to limit or retard actual scientific advance. "The difficulty in this position is not that it lacks ultimate philosophical justification. As so often happens, it is the polemical formulation that has the most impact. Like other forms of positivism, this position in administrative theory raises too bright a halo over linguistic purity. Pressing a complex world into easy dichotomies, it induces a premature abandonment of wide areas of experience to the world of the aesthetic, the metaphysical, the moral. Let us grant the premise that there is an ultimately irreducible nonrational (responsive) element in valuation, inaccessible to scientific appraisal. This cannot justify the judgment in a particular case that the anticipated irreducible element has actually been reached."[3]

(5) Logical positivism opens the door to action that is meaningless, irrational. A paradox is involved here. Logical positivism is a present-day extension of the rationalist tradition. Yet one writer has recently said of it:

"Rarely has a philosophy inspired by science afforded so much aid and comfort to the mystic." How does this come about? In this fashion: Logical positivism sharply separates fact and value. Values are unverifiable and hence not subject to scientific inquiry. The theory of value most closely associated with logical positivism is the emotive theory: expressions of value, of good and bad, right and wrong, are mere expressions of emotion, not genuine propositions. And all emotions stand equal before the bar of scientific enquiry. Sometimes logical positivists bow politely to the field of ethics, saying that they recognize its importance, though as scientists it is no matter of professional interest. It is difficult to see what the polite bow could really mean, however, in view of the basic postulates of logical positivism.

In any event the critic points to what he regards as anomalous: the rational becomes the servant of the irrational. The whole paraphernalia of reason and science are put into the service of purposes basically meaningless, beyond rational inquiry.

To this point the logical positivist would respond that he did not create the universe but must live with it as it is—as he finds it. (Logical positivism is usually associated with agnosticism. But some religious people also find it congenial; they fit their faith comfortably into the area of nonverifiable values.) If values cannot be verified, that is hardly his fault. What he offers is reason in the realization of human purposes, and this is as high an office as reason can attain.[4]

The Achievement of Goals

No solutions to the value problem in public administration have been given in this chapter. Nor were any intended, though the chapter may reflect unduly a personal judgment or bias against logical positivism. The aim was the more modest one of posing some of the problems, of sensitizing the student to the issues. The next generation of administrative students will be seeking to solve the problems, to resolve the issues. In this they will not be alone, and it is well to remember that public administration does not stand alone. It is woven into the whole fabric of social and intellectual life, and the development of thinking in public administration will be joined to developments in the other social sciences, in philosophy, and in society as a whole.

Let us close the chapter with a comment on one of the important questions: Does it make sense to study means to maximize goals "in general" apart from specification of particular goals? The answer to this is Yes and No. (1) As a logical and ethical matter, No. Logically, means are always relative to particular goals; there is no most efficient way to achieve all collective goals whatsoever. Ethically, means should always be weighed in relation to ends, and ends to means. (2) As a practical matter, Yes—over a large area of administrative study. Over a large area of administrative concern, the "lower" or "mechanical," one need not as a practical matter consider ends in each case, although he should do it occasionally both for particular cases and in the most generalized fashion he can. To hold otherwise would fatally inhibit the capacity to generalize, to learn from experience, to improve our capacity to achieve collective ends we all believe are important. Modern bureaucratic administration may not be—indeed is not—the most efficient means to achieve *any* cooperative goal. This is a static and culture-bound point of view. But it is an effective means of rational cooperation in achieving goals that we in modern Western society wish at the present time. In short, it is good for what it is good for. The question remains open whether there are still better ways of achieving present goals and still higher goals.

Footnotes to Chapter Six. The Value Problem in Administrative Study

1. From an unpublished manuscript, *Administration and Institutional Leadership*, by Philip Selznick.

2. Selznick, *op. cit.* At this point the attack is upon the logical-positivist *position*, but the philosophy has not yet been named and attacked directly, as it is below.

3. Selznick, *op. cit.*

4. For the statement of the logical-positivist position in the literature of public administration, see the works of Herbert A. Simon that have been cited above. One unfamiliar with the philosophical writings probably could have no better introduction than two small books, the first a classic statement of the position, the second an attempt to refute the first: A. J. Ayer, *Language, Truth and Logic*, first published in London in 1936; the current impression (New York, Dover Publications, Inc., 1953) is preferable to any early edition because of an added introduction; and C. E. M. Joad, *A Critique of Logical Positivism* (Chicago, University of Chicago Press, 1950).

chapter seven

Retrospect and Prospect

The study of administration began with the beginning of civilization and was closely involved therein. Civilization—the word is from the same root as "city"—implies increased density of population and increased complexity of life. Increased density of population requires a rise in the level of rational cooperation in order to sustain itself. Increased complexity of life implies an increase in rational cooperation and *necessitates* an increase in rational cooperation to make the goods of civilization commensurate with its inherent disadvantages. In other words, good administration can help make complexity yield returns in terms of diverse goods of life widely distributed.

In the course of history administration has sometimes reached high levels of performance, and administrative study has sometimes been seriously pursued. As we have seen, however, the past century witnessed a vast increase in the size, number, and complexity of administrative systems; and in the same period the study of administration entered a new phase. It became self-conscious, aware of administration as a general phenomenon, and eager to apply the methodology of science to the problem of making human cooperation more effective.

Let us return to an old perspective: The social sciences are not necessarily backward compared with the physical, as is customarily assumed. It is in large part certainly the vast increase in rational cooperation that has produced the wonders of physical science and technology. By common agreement, civilization, and perhaps even all life on this planet, stands in danger of destruction through another world war. If half the human race can be mustered and hurled in battle against the other half—to the destruction of both—this can be described as the utter negation of all morality; but morality apart, could it not be considered a great triumph of social science? Is not the modern nation-in-arms a marvel of rational cooperation?

This is written seriously, but yet in cynical jest. True, the accomplishments of social science are grossly underrated, and the social scientists are unfairly held responsible for the moral failures of society as a whole. But there are surely serious implications and limitations in the view that the social scientist is and should be scientist or technologist purely, with no concern for the ends of his endeavor; and there are limitations to rational cooperation when it lacks moral purposes beyond cooperation itself.

Public administration has been pictured in the preceding pages as a field of study that is growing rapidly, in ferment with new ideas, and challenged by major problems and opportunities. It will be useful to note briefly some of the present problems, challenges, and opportunities.

(1) An obvious challenge of the present is the integration of public administration with the other social sciences. Public administration in its early days had a natural drive toward self-sufficiency. But now the drive is outward and there is much to do. Many of the oncoming generation of students will find exciting careers in this enterprise. The rewards to public administration in the concepts, techniques, and insights of the various social sciences will be great; and there will be not just borrowing and adaptation, but *creative interchange*. For there is much to be learned from public administration, from the discipline and from the activity.

(2) An opportunity closely related to the preceding lies in rigorous empirical testing of beliefs and hypotheses concerning administrative behavior. For those with a bent for the laboratory there is much to be done in separating truth from falsehood, and in refining and sharpening what is known to be true but known only crudely. The psychological mechanisms of authority in organizations, the nature of administrative communications systems, the creation and maintenance of group value systems—these are but samples of the problem areas for research. Though what we have already accomplished in the area of rational cooperation deserves great respect—and any other attitude seems naïve and dangerous—great opportunities surely remain unexplored. Major break-throughs in theory and practice may yet be possible. Let us say they *are* possible.

(3) Related also to (1) but moving in a somewhat different direction is *model experimentation*—the application to administrative study of *all possible perspectives and metaphors*, so that their respective and comparative uses may be discovered. In the beginning—traditionally—public administration was seen through the eyes of the law, and was thought of primarily as a set of legal norms. From the Scientific Management movement came a great deal of mechanical metaphor: administrative systems were conceived as machines to be constructed for maximum efficiency. It seems obvious that both of these models or perspectives have a measure of truth and usefulness, but only a limited measure. Administration is nearly as broad as life, and it is a ready presumption that the whole gamut of perspectives and models that our culture provides should be explored and exploited in relation to administration.

(4) An obvious problem and challenge concerns the value problem. Here the administrative student is perhaps dependent ultimately upon major philosophic currents, but he has certainly an important interpretative task, and perhaps even a creative role of the second magnitude if not the first, in philosophy. Administration cannot be studied or practiced apart from the answers to the big questions. We deceive ourselves if we think so. It is not a question whether we *should* be interested in such things in our profession. Administration is at the center of our civilization, and it is the big questions that civilization is about, one way or another.

(5) Related to (4), and an important aspect of it, is the relationship of public administration (*a*) to the area of politics, in the sense of party and pressure-group activity, and (*b*) to the area of politics, in the sense of policy

creation. (These two are, of course, closely related, but not identical.) At present there is great confusion because of the abandonment of the politics-administration dichotomy. But there is also much interesting and original thinking. *This is and will continue to be for a long time one of the most significant areas of American political theory*, though one often overlooked by those who call themselves political theorists. The latter's interest should be solicited and their assistance if possible secured.

(6) Also related to (4) is the need to do much better than we have with the subjects of leadership and creativity. Our past history—the bent of the Scientific Management movement toward machine thinking, the practical need to sell public administration in terms of dollars and cents saved the taxpayer—led to too great a concentration on such matters as duplication and overlapping, stenographic pools, and paper-routing. We need not decry such interests. One can bleed to death through the capillaries. But there must be a complementary interest in institutional leadership and in how creativity can be built into administrative systems. For one can also die of cerebral hemorrhage—or walk in front of a bus.

(7) Related to (6) is the future of the public service. The whole complex of ideas associated with the term *civil service* needs to be rethought in the broadest, most imaginative terms. Our present amalgam of ideas, derived from such native sources as the Scientific Management movement and such foreign sources as the British Civil Service, is surely inadequate to the present demands upon American government. We have just scratched the surface of institutional invention in this area. This type of rethinking is illustrated by Norton E. Long's essay, "Public Policy and Administration: The Goals of Rationality and Responsibility."[1]

(8) Various areas of contemporary administrative study hold promise of exciting work and rich rewards. One of these is the field of comparative administration, which has developed as an interest in the past decade as a result of the enlargement of American interests in war, cold war, and reconstruction and technical assistance. This is an area of academic study—and one in which the rewards of working with other social sciences are especially great; but it is also an area of action.[2] American students of administration are currently scattered about the world on study and technical-assistance missions.

Another obvious bustling frontier is the case method in public administration. One challenge here is so to develop the techniques that the cases can perform an educational need now unfulfilled: that of conveying a sense of the nature and importance of administration to great numbers of people who see it only as dull routine or technical matter for technicians only. Such people quite literally do not know what their lives depend on; and this is a serious—conceivably fatal—cultural lag.

(9) There is the challenge which at the risk of overstatement and ridicule can be called that of developing an administrative culture. This means first of all further development of present knowledge and techniques, and secondly it means the broadening of interests in administration, and the weaving of it together with other fields of knowledge—including ultimately philosophy and religion. Thirdly it means the imaginative reconstruction of

administrative or bureaucratic institutions, the building-in of leadership and creativity, and adjustment to our collective ideas and ideals as these unfold. Fourthly it means a much wider spread of knowledge about administration. This last is essential if we are to avoid a managerial society and realize our democratic ideals in a complex world. Administration should be thought of primarily not as what a few do to the many by virtue of superior knowledge (though there may always be an inevitable amount of that), but rather as modern rules of the game, a game which all play in various ways and with varying skill.[3]

In conclusion we may well return to a question posed in the preface, namely, Who should study public administration? The answer to this question is: Everyone—but in varying ways and with varying intensity. The basic reason is *understanding*. All people in a civilized society need an appreciation of the role of administration in their culture because, willy-nilly, administration is an important aspect of their lives, from the nearest physical aspect to the remotest spiritual or intellectual aspect. *All* persons in a civilized society are consumers of administration, and they should be *good* consumers, prepared to react intelligently and appreciatively, or with intelligent criticism.

Nearly all persons in a civilized society are also participants in administration, in varying degree and manner. And *according to degree and manner* they need to know what has been learned about administration, that is to say, the technical or professional lore. For some this can be a brief and easy learning experience. For others it can only be a protracted and arduous professional course of training.

Public administration as a discipline has entered into a period of wide interchange and exploration. The avenues for exciting work that it offers both in study and practice open in all directions. The aptest words to conclude with are perhaps these: If the demands of present world civilization are met, administrative thought must establish a working relationship with every major province in the realm of human learning.

Footnotes to Chapter Seven. Retrospect and Prospect

1. In *Public Administration Review*, Winter 1952, 22–31.

2. See "Notes on Literature Available for the Study of Comparative Administration" by Fred Riggs, *American Political Science Review* 48:515–537 (1954) for an introduction to the literature.

3. In this connection see the recently published *The Human Enterprise Process* (University, University of Alabama Press, 1954) by William Brownrigg. This is an analysis of the "enterprise process"—roughly what we have called rational cooperation—which displays people alternately playing deciding, executing, and utilizing roles.

Bibliographical Note

The following bibliographical items are selected as best designed to open up the field of public administration and to enable anyone, but especially the newcomer, to see the field—its development, its main concepts, its major concerns and divisions, its present trends and present periphery. Items included are not necessarily good in any abstract sense, but may be good for the purpose.

There are first of all the general textbooks. *Introduction to the Study of Public Administration* (3rd ed., New York, The Macmillan Co., 1948) by L. D. White has been standard for a generation. Two recently published general texts are: *Public Administration* (New York, Rinehart & Company, Inc., 1953) by M. E. Dimock and Gladys O. Dimock, and *Public Administration* (New York, The Ronald Press Company, 1953) by John M. Pfiffner and R. Vance Presthus. The contents of these two books is reviewed in Chapter Three. The most recent textbook is *Management in the Public Service* (New York, McGraw-Hill Book Company, Inc., 1954) by John D. Millett. It is somewhat narrower in focus than the customary textbook, concentrating on management.

Other general textbooks in print are: *Public Administration in a Democratic Society* (Boston, D. C. Heath & Company, 1950) by W. Brooke Graves; *Governmental Administration* (New York, Harper & Brothers, 1951) by James C. Charlesworth; and *Elements of Public Administration* (New York, Prentice-Hall, Inc., 1946) edited by Fritz Morstein Marx.

In the field of personnel administration, *Public Personnel Administration* (3rd ed., New York, Harper & Brothers, 1950) by William E. Mosher, J. D. Kingsley, and O. Glenn Stahl has long been standard.

There are three books of readings which cover the general field of public administration: *Administration: The Art and Science of Organization and Management* (New York, Alfred A. Knopf, Inc., 1949) by Albert Lepawsky; *Public Administration: Readings and Documents* (New York, Rinehart & Company, Inc., 1951) by Felix A. Nigro; and *Ideas and Issues in Public Administration* (New York, McGraw-Hill Book Company, Inc., 1953) by Dwight Waldo. The emphasis of each is suggested in the titles.

There are a number of essays of the nature of general surveys of developments or trends which should prove helpful. Four of these essays constitute a single series as follows: "Trends in the Theory of Public Administration," *Public Administration Review* 10:161–168 (Summer, 1950) by John M. Gaus; "Trends of a Decade in Administrative Practices," *Public Administration Review* 10:229–235 (Autumn, 1950) by Charles S. Ascher; "Trends of a Decade in Administrative Values," *Public Administration Review* 11:1–9 (Winter, 1951) by Wallace S. Sayre; and "Trends in Teaching Public Administration," *Public Administration Review* 12:69–77 (Spring, 1950) by George A. Graham.

Among recent trends essays are also: "The Scope of Public Administration," *Western Political Quarterly* 5:124–137 (1952) by Marver H. Bernstein; "The Study of Public Administration in the United States," *Public Administration* 29:131–143 (1951) by W. J. M. Mackenzie (this is a British publication); *American Administrative Theory* (Lawrence, Kansas, 1950) by E. O. Stene; and "Political Science and Public Administration: A Note on the State of the Union," *American Political Science Review* 46:660–676 (1952) by Roscoe C. Martin.

Two publications of the author also come under this heading: *The Administrative State: A Study of the Political Theory of American Public Administration* (New York, The Ronald Press Company, 1948); and "Administrative Theory in the United States: A Survey and Prospect," *Political Studies* 2:70–86 (1954).

On education and training, see *Education for Public Administration* (Chicago, Social Science Research Council, Committee on Public Administration, 1941) by George A. Graham. This is now somewhat outdated, but an excellent work. See also *Public Service and University Education* (Princeton, Princeton University Press, 1949) edited by Joseph McLean.

Among books significant in demonstrating some recent trends see *Administrative Behavior: A Study of Decision-Making Processes in Administrative Organization* (New York, The Macmillan Co., 1947) by Herbert A. Simon; *Public Administration and Policy Development* (New York, Harcourt, Brace & Company, 1952) edited by Harold Stein; *Reflections on Public Administration* (University, University of Alabama Press, 1947) by John M. Gaus; *Bureaucracy in a Democracy* (New York, Harper & Brothers, 1950) by Charles S. Hyneman; *Morality and Administration in Democratic Government* (Baton Rouge, Louisiana State University Press, 1952) by Paul H. Appleby; *New Horizons in Public Administration: A Symposium* (University, University of Alabama Press, 1945) by L. D. White *et al.*; *Policy and Administration* (University, University of Alabama Press, 1949) by Paul H. Appleby; *Politics, Economics and Welfare* (New York, Harper & Brothers, 1953) by Robert A. Dahl and Charles E. Lindblom.

Two older books, but classics, are: *Papers on the Science of Administration* (New York, Institute of Public Administration, 1937) edited by Luther Gulick and Lyndall Urwick; and *The Frontiers of Public Administration* (Chicago, University of Chicago Press, 1933) by John M. Gaus, L. D. White, and Marshall Dimock.

A good survey (but now somewhat outdated) with special emphasis upon research is *Research in Public Administration* (Chicago, Social Science Research Council, Committee on Public Administration, 1945) by William Anderson and John M. Gaus.

A newcomer can get an excellent sense of the status and progress of the discipline from the files of *Public Administration Review*.

Finally, two bibliographies. One is the standard general bibliography: *Bibliography on Public Administration—Annotated* (4th ed., Washington, American University Press, 1953) by Catheryn Seckler-Hudson. The other concerns the human relations approach, and demonstrates the impact of materials from psychology and related fields: *Human Relations in Public Administration* (Chicago, Public Administration Service, 1949) by Alfred De Grazia.

PB 11128

Date Due

JAN 1 9 '67			
Feb 22			
APR 1 5 '69			

Demco 293-5